Difficult Questions On Dinosaurs

(Answered By a Creationist)

By Richard B. Pittack, B.A., M. Div.

Difficult Questions on Dinosaurs
By Richard B. Pittack.

Published by Walden's Computer Services.

Printing History:
February 2008. First edition.

Title: Difficult Questions on Dinosaurs
ID: 1951204
ISBN: 978-0-615-19991-7

Contents

Difficult Questions on Dinosaurs

(Answered by a Creationist)

The Evidence for Evolution is *not* overwhelming

By

Richard B. Pittack, B.A., M. Divinity

"When the queen of Sheba heard of Solomon's fame, she came to Jerusalem to test him with hard questions. Arriving with a very great caravan – with camels carrying spices, large quantities of gold, and precious stones – she came to Solomon and talked with him about all she had on her mind. Solomon answered all her questions; nothing was too hard for him to explain to her."

NIV

2 Chronicles 9:1-2

INTRODUCTION

Dear Readers,

Unfortunately, I was not granted the Wisdom of Solomon for my meetings on dinosaurs. I suppose Solomon was able to answer the queen of Sheba and her "hard questions" with relative ease. The hard questions submitted to the "DINOSAUR QUESTION BOX" I read with thought and some of them would take several days of reflection and consideration before formulating my answer.

This book is not the typical "questions and answers on dinosaurs" book. It is not a book for children enabling them to find out the largest recorded dinosaur, to discover what dinosaurs ate or even how they managed to get up after naptime. An informative book on the biology and anatomy of the "mighty reptiles" – it is not except in rare cases where these two features were part of the clarity necessary for an answer to a particular question.

The series of questions in this treatise of answers has arisen from meetings conducted on dinosaurs. The questions have come from all kinds of people in various and sundry walks of life. Some of the questions were common and not much is to be learned from answers to such generalities. However, some of the questions are not only posited by the curious but come from hearts filled with consternation while contemplating the subject of theodicy ("Derived from the two Greek words meaning 'deity' and 'justice.' This is an attempt to justify the goodness of God in the face of a manifold evil present in the world." See *a Handbook of Theological Terms* by Van A. Harvey, Pp.236-241).

Did God create such monsters? Did the Creator actually contribute to the world's landscape of tooth and claw? Is the canvass of God's creation not only etched in blood but filled with the stench and smell emanating from the so-called Mesozoic Era of the past? I only hope and pray these questions were adequately answered and people were helped to see the solutions of certain troubling issues. Perhaps finding the answers to these same questions as well as discovering answers to their own questions will also help some of my readers.

Holding meetings was a great learning experience for me. I was amazed by the number of people who do not believe in the existence of dinosaurs. I suppose this was a counterbalance belief to the idea of the cruel and vicious nature of predatory dinosaurs or not being able to place the creation of dinosaurs in the proper framework of biblical history and making the problem disappear by dispensing with dinosaurs, altogether. I was also surprised at people I met, who could not accept the fact: certain dinosaurs were meat-eaters. They actually believed there were no carnivorous dinosaurs and that all of them were herbivorous.

There are other belief systems that not only amazed me but also troubled my heart. For example, people rejecting the Universal Flood of the Bible and accepting the Noachian Flood as a mere local flood occurring in Mesopotamia. But the most dangerous and unsettling idea fostered among a few believers in the Bible, is the false notion that dinosaurs were the offspring of humans uniting with animals.

You will notice, in some of my responses to questions, I am in disagreement with my fellow creationists. For examples, I don't believe that *Parasaurolophus* (an herbivorous duck-billed dinosaur) breathed fire; *Tyrannosaurus rex* ate watermelons; "dragons" in the Bible should be automatically translated as "dinosaurs"; the *Behemoth* of Job 41 [A mythological *sea creature*] should be interpreted as a *land dinosaur* and that there are living dinosaurs such as Mokele-mbembe (a sauropod supposed to be living in Africa). Also, material viewed by many creationists as supporting the cause of creationism, I view as unscientific and remain skeptical of such information. For example, the discovery of dinosaurian track ways with man's footprints at the Paluxy River site in Texas. When the facts are truly investigated and analyzed, the contemporaneous existence of man and dinosaurs, in this case, is simply not a bona fide argument for a young earth.

This book has no chapter divisions. Each question and answer will serve as its own chapter. Also, after each question there are brackets. Within each bracket is an explanation as to the source of the question. The DINOSAUR QUESTION BOX is a container I prepared for the meetings. On the outside of the cardboard box, there were colorful pictures of dinosaurs with a slot cut out in the top. It was placed in the foyer and the audience could drop off their questions whenever they wanted. I would take the questions home in order to select the best ones. Rather than explain the meeting procedures, I will let you read what is written in the brackets. In some cases, my actions and emotions during meeting time, are explained beneath the part entitled ANSWER.

I was fortunate enough to be invited to several churches and private and public schools. I will never forget the caliber of young people who helped me with the programs. They placed my dinosaur models in strategic areas; made certain that the microphones were set up and even asked if they might run my precious collection of dinosaur slides. The kids also broke the ice with a new audience, breaking down my fears and securing my confidence.

The final point worth mentioning: I was impressed with the questions that were submitted. Many of the questions were well formulated and spoke to the serious nature of the issue at hand. I am convinced that such meetings were beneficial to the public. *God as Creator is very much a part of the gospel.* Simply ask John the Revelator who wrote:

"Then I saw another angel flying in mid-air and he had the *eternal gospel* to proclaim to those who live on the earth – to every nation, tribe, language and people. He said with a loud voice, *Fear God* and give him glory, because the hour of his judgment has come. *Worship him who made the heavens, the earth, the sea and the springs of water.*"

NIV

Revelation 14:6-7

(See also Exodus 20:8-11)

Respectfully,

Richard B. Pittack

Palmdale, California

September 9, 2007

P.S.

Evolutionary scientists and teachers love to poke fun at creationists, who believe that man and dinosaurs lived contemporaneously. Such scientists and teachers love to point to the cartoons, which illustrate Fred Flintstone and dinosaurs living side by side; love to talk about the "yabba-dabba-doo" science of those creationists, who believe that man and dinosaurs originated on the sixth day of the literal week of biblical Creation.

Readers, who hold to the theory that man and dinosaurs were separated by millions of years, ought to first read the ANSWERS to QUESTIONS 33-36. This will give you some idea that the scientific theories regarding measurement of time (chronology), are not accurate enough to escape challenge of the methods used for "deep time" as is supposedly recorded in the Geological Column. I say, "Some idea" since the answers to questions 33-36, are for the most part, not the fullest and complete answers that could be stated. There is a host of reasons given by creationists, other than those I have mentioned, for the belief that dinosaurs and men existed side by side.

FORMAT I

QUESTIONS ASKED BY CREATIONISTS

BEFORE THE FLOOD

QUESTION ONE:

DID DINOSAURS ROAM THE EARTH BEFORE THE GREAT BIBLICAL FLOOD?

ANSWER:

[A member of the audience, who placed it in the DINOSAUR QUESTION BOX, wrote this first question. This query I answered directly in my meeting. But remember! I am trying to do two things at the same time – go back in time and speak to the audience while at the same moment addressing my readers. Very rarely did I read quotes to my living audience. The quotes are for you – the readers]

Dinosaurs had to be a part of the original creation. Therefore, they roamed this planet for at least sixteen hundred years before the time of the Flood mentioned in the book of Genesis. "Roaming the earth" is proper terminology since in the first place, science has determined (and with very good reasons) dinosaurs to be land animals and not swamp creatures:

"These [giants] were terrestrial rather than sea dwellers, and their huge limbs and stumpy toes gave more than a passing resemblance to the heavy pachydermal mammals. [These giants refer to the species that Richard Owen singled out – *Iguanodon, Megalosaurus and Hylaeosaurus*]

"These characters, coupled with the enormous size of the beasts, were 'deemed sufficient ground for establishing, a distinct tribe or sub-order of saurian reptiles', proclaimed Owen, 'for which I would propose the name *Dinosauria.*' Dinosaur means literally 'terrible lizard', a suitably evocative title given in recognition of the creature's dimensions and undoubted ferocity."

The Hot-Blooded Dinosaur

Adrian J. Desmond

P.14

Richard Owen was a creationist and Desmond gives the *ulterior motive* for Owen's proposal of the name *Dinosauria.* Not only did Owen believe these forms were the *Crown of Reptilian Creation* but:

"The superiority of the dinosaurs, living in a glorious 'age of reptiles,' was a direct act of divine creation. Species did not transmute into one another but were placed on the earth by design and if they appeared to form a succession, it was a result of divine planning rather than evolution."

[Ibid. P.17]

[Readers should understand that Adrian J. Desmond, the author of the above paragraph, does not agree with the philosophy of Owen. In fact, he definitely opposes divine creation and design]

Genesis 1:24-27 states that *man and land animals were created on the sixth day*. All animals, including the dinosaur, *roamed the earth* prior to the Flood and many of them right up until the time of the Flood [Some of the species representing the dinosaur "kind" were taken into the Ark (Genesis 6:19). Therefore, some of them *roamed the earth* even *after the Flood*]

In the second place, the majority of the dinosaur kingdoms perished in the Flood; *dinosaur graveyards attest to this fact*. If most of the dinosaurs perished in the Flood, then they must have been *roaming the earth* at the *time of the Great Flood and prior to it*. Before leaving QUESTION ONE, the following quote contrasts creation and evolution on the subject of *dinosaur origins*:

"Evolutionists claim that dinosaurs evolved from some reptile that had originally evolved from amphibians. However, they cannot point to any transitional (in-between) forms to substantiate their argument. Dinosaur family trees in evolutionary books show many distinct types of dinosaurs, but only hypothetical lines join them up to some common ancestor. The lines are dotted because there is no fossil evidence. Evolutionists simply cannot prove their belief in a non-dinosaur ancestor for dinosaurs."

The Revised & Expanded Answers Book

Edited by Don Batten, Ph.D.

Ken Ham*Jonathan Sarfati*Carl Wieland

P.241

QUESTION TWO:
HOW OLD ARE DINOSAURS?

ANSWER:

[This question was also from the DINOSAUR QUESTION BOX. I was surprised by the present tense "are." This is another question answered during a public meeting]

Notice the present tense "are". Actually, no dinosaurs are living now unless you want to argue the alleged sightings made in Africa, which seem to be describing a giant sauropod. This giant exists only by word of mouth and is named *Mokele-Mbembe*. The phenomenon is no different from the reports of the *Loch Ness Monster* except in this case, it is set in Africa. The giant is alleged to be haunting the Likouala swamp of the People's Republic of the Congo, right in the extreme depths of the continent (Jacobs – *Quest for the African Dinosaur*, P.245). I am convinced *this story belongs to science fiction or pseudo science.* [For further insight into Mokele-Mbembe; readers are to refer to the answer given for QUESTION TWENTY-NINE]

I can take this question also to mean *how old are dinosaur bones?* Many creationists contend the oldest bone does not go back more than six thousand years. The main body of dinosaurs was destroyed in the Noachian Flood. At that time, they were in existence for about 1,656 years. Many died after their release from the Ark and following the Ararat migration. Hundreds of years later, the remnant of dinosaurs most likely died from cold weather brought on by the Ice Age.

I have another question from THE DINOSAUR QUESTION BOX. It is similar to the question just answered.

QUESTION THREE:

HOW OLD WERE DINOSAURS WHEN THEY PERISHED IN THE FLOOD?

ANSWER:

[This answer was also stated in my meetings and followed question two. Sometimes, I did not take the questions home. I answered them at the meeting but I always drew more than one question from the box, just in case the answer required too much thought time, the question was too complex to answer, and, heaven forbid! – I DIDN'T KNOW THE ANSWER to one of the questions. When I got better at it, I was brave enough to have an assistant pass the microphone throughout the audience. I never said, "I don't know the answer" but the audience could always tell the difference between a learned response and a beat-around-the-bush response. To this day, I do not know if I wasn't as expert in the topic as I thought I was or if the audience had been reading up on the subject of dinosaurs and was prepared to ask me some rather difficult questions when they attended the meetings. I would go home at night and read all the questions in the QUESTION BOX. A few questions, I figured would take the allotted time of the ten minutes allowed for answers, and I saved those particular questions for key nights. You will see such a plan develop as I continue to answer the questions in this book]

I assume that the dinosaurs could be found in different growth patterns and, therefore, were of different ages. For example:

*Some were in the *form of eggs.* As far as we know, dinosaurs did not give birth to living forms. Rather, they laid eggs. However, it is quite possible that some species of dinosaurs gave live birth.

*Some dinosaurs were in the *form of hatchlings*; others were in the *form of juveniles.*

*Still others were *mature or old.* It may be that some types of dinosaurs were *like reptiles* in that their *cells were continually replaced.* If so, the theory claims these particular dinosaurs would have lived longer and longer. It was this continued growth that is believed to have actually helped the dinosaurs extend their longevity.

Paleontologists have deduced that the dinosaurs, *Maiasaura,* doubled their birth weight each year until adulthood was reached within the short space of *four years.* This means that *a fourteen-inch hatchling became a thirty-foot adult* in the same amount of time (Lessem – *Kings of Creation*). Growth rings found in the bone structure of some species indicated that they could have lived for *at least 120 years.* Some claim dinosaurs had lived a relatively slow-paced lifestyle and could have lived *for centuries.*

Thomas E. Svarney and Patricia Barnes-Svarney write:

"Scientists do not know the exact lifespan of the dinosaurs, but they estimate that dinosaurs lived about 75 to 300 years. This educated guess is based on examining the microstructure of dinosaur bones, which indicate that the dinosaurs matured slowly."

The Handy Dinosaur Answer Book

P.269

Again, this question may also be intended to mean *how old was the Dinosaurian Kingdoms at the time of the flood*? The Flood came upon this earth approximately 1,656 years after the creation of the world. You can, from the Bible, trace the human genealogical data of the Hebrew text that gives the birthdays of each named son but, of course, you have to assume the unreasonable probability of having each named son being born on the exact birthday of his father (SDA Commentary, Vol.1). This scale of years shows that the flood came in the 1,656[th] year from creation or A.M. ("in the year of the world") 1656. The dinosaurs were created on the 6th day along with all the other land animals. Therefore, in 1656, the Dinosaurian Kingdoms were less than 2000 years old.

DURING THE FLOOD

QUESTION FOUR:

I AM A CHRISTIAN AND BELIEVE IN THE OLD AND NEW TESTAMENTS OF THE CHRISTIAN BIBLE BUT I DO NOT BELIEVE IN A WORLD WIDE FLOOD WHICH IS SUPPOSEDLY RESPONSIBLE FOR THE BURIAL OF THE DINOSAURS AND THEIR EXTINCTION. WASN'T THE BIBLE FLOOD JUST A LOCAL FLOOD THAT TOOK PLACE IN MESOPOTAMIA?

ANSWER:

[This fourth question did not come from the DINOSAUR QUESTION BOX; neither did the audience propose it. This was an anticipated question, which I dealt with either in a sermon or in one of my lectures]

I would urge you to make your decision based on biblical logic. This is the only way for Bible students to know if the Flood was local or worldwide.

Genesis, chapters 1-11, is considered to be a literary unit. More than this, the chapters are in a *Universal Context*. The creation story has God making all things on the earth. There is nothing that God did not make. Thus, there is a *universal creation theme* (John 1:1-3).

Then, there is the theme of the *fall*. Since all humans have sinned and fallen, not just some: sin created *universal problems* (Romans 5:12-14). Also, *salvation is universal* (John 3:16) in the sense that salvation is provided for all men and not that everyone will be saved since they have free will and can choose the wrong way. The promise of salvation, through the offered covenant, is for all people that would inhabit the entire earth, *another universal theme* (Hebrews 10:26-31). Finally, it is in the middle of these universal themes that the story of the Flood appears (Genesis 6-9). Clearly, it would be inconsistent and inappropriate to extract the Flood story from the rest of Genesis 1-11 and say that it has *only a local meaning*. The reason that God brought the Flood in the first place was to exercise *universal judgment* against a *universal problem of wickedness* that had spread throughout the earth. Genesis 6:12 state "And God looked upon the earth, and behold; it was corrupt; for all flesh had corrupted his way upon the earth." It would be illogical to conclude these words apply only to a local situation in Mesopotamia.

Here are some issues to think through:

*The enormous size of the Ark. The length of the Ark was about 150 yards long, 75 feet wide and 45 feet high (Genesis 6:15).

*The mountains that the Flood covered (Genesis 7:20).

*The mass of the collected animals that entered the Ark (Genesis 7:2-3).

All three of these issues certainly contradict a local flood theory and *affirm the truth of a Universal Flood.* For example, why was the Ark built with such large dimensions if only the animals of Mesopotamia were to be considered? Again, the mountains covered by the Flood include those of Ararat. The highest peak is 17,000 feet.

Water of such volume, as to cover a mountain over three miles high, cannot logically be viewed in a Mesopotamian local flood context. Finally, a huge gathering of animals was brought into the Ark to preserve animal species for the future. The reason for this is specifically stated in Genesis 7:4, "I will cause it to rain upon the earth ... every living substance that I have made will I destroy from off the face of the earth." It would seem incredible to view this reason given for the gathering of animals as applying to only a local flood situation in Mesopotamia.

The Scriptures lend no support for the view of some religious scientists and liberal theologians, who attempt to reduce the Flood to a local inundation, primarily affecting Mesopotamia. To treat the Flood as having been less than worldwide is to put a superficial spin on the biblical record of this catastrophe.

In Genesis, chapters 6-9, there are *more than thirty expressions describing the universality of the Flood and its effects.* A number of these expressions will be examined:

*Genesis 6:13 – "And God said unto Noah, the end of all flesh is come before me; for the earth is filled with violence through them; and, behold, I will destroy them with the earth." Such ends could not possibly be accomplished unless the Bible statements were intended to denote a World Wide Flood rather than a local. Already it has been stated: a universal flood necessitated the building of a huge Ark to preserve representatives of all the created kinds of animals for the future world. If the Flood were to be a mere regional inundation in Mesopotamia, then such a type Ark would have been completely unnecessary. Noah would simply have taken his family and, along with the animals, migrated to other regions.

*Genesis 6:17 - "And behold, I, even I, do bring a flood of waters upon the earth, to destroy all flesh, wherein is the breath of life, from under heaven; and everything that is in the earth shall die." Again, God is placing great emphasis on the Flood as Universal. He is not threatening to bring a little local flood into Mesopotamia but rather a Universal Flood upon the earth. The Flood would not be a destructive element for a few animal species in a local area but for all animal species upon the earth and under heaven. Genesis 7:1, 3 give support to this suggestion – "And the Lord said unto Noah, come thou ... into the ark ... take ... fowls also of the air ... to keep seed alive upon the face of all the earth."

Such an invitation to Noah and command to take birds into the ark would be irrelevant if the Flood were to be only local. The words have significance only in the light of a Universal Flood. If the flood were merely local, then what would have prevented birds from flying out of Mesopotamia and into other regions to preserve their seed? Also "to keep seed alive upon the face of all the earth" could only mean the birds taken into the Ark, after their release, would repopulate the earth with avian species. This would be accomplished by the power of variation within their gene pools and eventual migration to all global regions.

*Genesis 7:11 – "… all the fountains of the great deep [were] broken up, and all the windows of heaven were opened." Few individuals truly realize the enormous geophysical implication of this event and it is difficult to imagine how anyone could read into these words a local flood rather than a universal one. This text vividly describes the Flood as a World Wide, cataclysmic event and tells of its power and destruction. The forces involved are certainly beyond man's imagination. The following statement helps man's mind to visualize the impressive nature of the Flood. It is but a small excerpt from White's chapter on "The Flood" but nevertheless it gives us some idea of the destructive and violent nature of the event:

"But upon the eighth day, dark clouds overspread the heavens. There followed the muttering of thunder and the flash of lightning. Soon large drops of rain began to fall. The world had never witnessed anything like this, and the hearts of men were struck with fear. All were secretly inquiring, 'Can it be that Noah was in the right, and that the world is doomed to destruction?' Darker and darker grew the heavens, and faster came the falling rain. The beasts were roaming about in the wildest terror, and their discordant cries seemed to moan out their own destiny and the fate of man. Then 'the fountains of the great deep were broken up, and the windows of heaven were opened.' Water appeared to come down from the clouds in mighty cataracts. Rivers broke away from their boundaries, and overflowed the valleys. Jets of water burst from the earth with indescribable force, throwing massive rocks hundreds of feet into the air, and these, in falling, buried themselves deep in the ground."

Patriarchs and Prophets

E.G. White

P.99

One cannot examine the earth and its geology without witnessing the physical evidence for the biblical Flood. A local flood theory simply does not fit the geological evidence. On the other hand there is overwhelming confirmation for a World Wide Flood. Randall W. Younker makes this observation:

"Massive concentrations of various fossilized animals in all sections of the earth attest to a sudden and enormous destruction of life globally. Many fossilized animals are standing upright, some with food in their mouths, indicating sudden submersion in mudslides, others are crushed or dismembered as by masses of violently moving earth. Extensive valleys and plains are veritable graveyards for the chaotic accumulation of creatures that died suddenly and together. All this far-ranging and nearly simultaneous destruction of life accords easily with the Flood account in Genesis. The physical evidence is not fabricated nor the Bible record exaggerated."

Gods Creation Looking at the Biblical Account

[Adult Sabbath School Bible Study Guide Teachers Edition]

P.107

Younker's statement indicates the fossils alone are powerful evidence for a World Wide Flood. There are, however, many other visible proofs of a Universal Catastrophe will be mentioned in later portions of this book.

*Genesis 7:18-22 - "And the waters prevailed, and were increased greatly upon the earth; and the ark went upon the face of the waters. And the waters prevailed exceedingly upon the earth; and all the high hills that were under the whole heaven, were covered. Fifteen cubits upward did the waters prevail; and the mountains were covered. And all flesh died that moved upon the earth, both of fowl, and of cattle, and of beast, and of every creeping thing that creepeth upon the earth, and every man: All in whose nostrils was the breath of life, of all that was in the dry land, died."

Certainly, these verses do not allude to a local flood situation in Mesopotamia. They set forth only one idea and the words could not be clearer; the biblical Flood would be of such great extent, the entire earth would be inundated.

What is more; not only would the hills of Mesopotamia be covered with water but the high hills under the whole heaven. This can be understood to specify that no hills under the skies would escape flooding and submersion. Finally, death-judgment was not for a handful of individuals in Mesopotamia but was to come upon all mankind upon the face of the globe. Everything on dry land was to be wiped out. The entire earth was to be cleansed of the corruption with the global bath from heaven. All life – including mankind and beast – would die as a result of the Great Flood.

One more passage will be considered.

*Genesis 9:13-15 – "I do set my bow in the cloud, and it shall be a token of a covenant between me and the earth. And it shall come to pass, when I bring a cloud over the earth, that the bow shall be seen in the cloud: And I will remember my covenant, which is between me and you and every living creature of all flesh; and the waters shall no more become a flood to destroy all flesh."

God's promise and its memory were to be perpetuated throughout the entire earth. It was not meant alone, for a handful of humans in Mesopotamia. The promise that God would not again bring a flood upon the earth was a Universal Promise made evident through the Universal Sign of the Rainbow.

If God intended His promise to be local rather than Universal, then the promise has been broken numerous times. Local flooding has never been halted in any region of the earth. Also, if the Flood were local, then the promise would have had a local intent. But the rainbow sign has been extended throughout the whole earth, proving the sign to be universal and thus the Flood to be Universal:

"It was God's purpose that as the children of after-generations should ask the meaning of the glorious arch which spans the heavens, their parents should repeat the story of the flood, and tell them that the Most High had bended the bow, and placed it in the clouds as an assurance that the waters should never again overflow the earth. Thus from generation to generation it would testify of divine love to man, and would strengthen his confidence in God."

Patriarchs and Prophets

E.G. White
Pp.106-107

In summary, this answer has been replete with responses to the question of the biblical Flood being local or universal. It is evident that the Flood was universal based on biblical logic. It is virtually unfeasible to believe in the Bible and at the same time endorse the local flood theory. The wording alone of Genesis 6-9 indicates a Universal Flood and not a local river overflow. To make the Flood local is to compromise with evolutionary biology and that geology based on the Doctrine of Uniformity.

QUESTION FIVE:

DID NOAH TAKE DINOSAURS INTO THE ARK AT THE TIME OF THE FLOOD?

ANSWER:

[This is an excellent question. I decided to answer it in the allotted 10 minutes on a special night. Of course, the following is an *extension of the answer* I gave to the live audience. Thus the reader, at least, benefits from *this book answer*, which is my intention]

I want you to know at the outset; there are no airtight answers in this matter since all creationists have a right to their own viewpoint when it comes to the subject of dinosaurs.

I am going to refer to statements made by a number of authors who are creationists. It will be interesting for us to note that the points of view will not be in total agreement. After sharing these opinions with you, I will give my personal perspective. Let us remember, our salvation is not dependent upon a correct answer to the question: were dinosaurs taken into the ark at the time of the Great Flood? However, it is a fair question, why not deal with it?

The first set of statements is in the juvenile book written by John Morris and Ken Ham illustrated by Jonathan Chong:

"God told Noah that some of *every* kind of land animal would come into the ark (Genesis 6:19) …

"First of all, I do not think God would have brought the biggest, oldest dinosaurs on the ark. He probably sent strong, young ones that would have babies after the flood. Remember that many dinosaurs were not very large when they were grown, and all of them were small when they were young.

"Secondly, although there were many different dinosaur names, there may have been fewer than fifty kinds of dinosaurs. Creation scientists from ICR [Institute for Creation Research] have shown that there was plenty of room in the ark for all the kinds of animals God sent Noah."

What Really Happened to the Dinosaurs? (1998)

P.22

Let us break this down:

Morris and Ham believe that Genesis 6:19 includes the *dinosaur land animals* in the word "every." They reason, how could Noah have followed God's instructions if the dinosaurs were left off the ark? The biggest and oldest were left out but *younger and stronger animals represented their kinds.* Morris and Ham contend that although dinosaurs had many different names, there may have been fewer than fifty kinds of dinosaurs. I take their argument to mean that all the kinds of dinosaurs were taken into the ark but *not every species.* Within each kind of dinosaur, there were variations made possible by genetic gene pools. Not every variation was taken on board but certainly, it is implied, all the major kinds of dinosaurs *were taken.*

David Unfred writes the next statement:

"At the time of the great worldwide flood, God told us that he saved ALL kinds of air-breathing land animals on the ark (Genesis 7:15). Does this mean that dinosaurs were on Noah's ark? Yes, at least one pair of each kind of dinosaur was on the ark – God said so, and He cannot lie."

Dinosaurs and the Bible (1990)

P.9 (Juvenile Book)

Unfred agrees with Morris and Ham. Yes, dinosaur kinds were taken into Noah's Ark at the time of the Great Flood but not every species. Noah would have a difficult problem in establishing the original kinds due to variation but God called the dinosaurs into the ark and He would have no trouble in His choice and selection. [Pittack's Note: To jump from the idea that God saved "ALL kinds of land breathing land animals on the ark" to "at least one pair of each kind of dinosaur" seems to be a misunderstanding of what the verse implies]

The third statement is from a juvenile book written by Paul S. Taylor:

"Noah did not have to go out and find the animals. God brought each one. This probably included a young pair of each main type of dinosaur. Perhaps God just included the basic kinds of dinosaurs, He first created; not every variety that had developed since creation."

The Great Dinosaur Mystery and the Bible (1987)

P.32

Again, there is agreement between the writers of these juvenile books; all major types of dinosaurs were taken into the ark. That is, all the kinds of dinosaurs. However, he goes on to write "… not every variety that had been developed since creation." I take this to mean: all the kinds of dinosaurs were taken into the ark but *not every species.* Thus Taylor is in *exact* agreement with Morris and Ham. Taylor also claims Genesis 7:15-16 to be the basis of his conclusion.

[Special Note: I have a strong feeling these writers borrowed from each other since they all reached the *same wrong conclusion.* Paul S. Taylor led off with the idea, followed by David Unfred; finally, followed by John Morris and Ken Ham. *To conclude that ALL kinds of land animals infer the exact same thing as ALL kinds of dinosaurs is jumping to the wrong conclusion.* For example, the dinosaur was a land animal whose kind was well represented on the ark but that does not infer this particular land animal had to have ALL OF ITS KIND represented on the ark]

I find myself to be more agreement with my fellow creationist, Frank Lewis Marsh, who wrote in 1967 (20 years prior to Paul S. Taylor):

"As the creator looked ahead and saw these postdiluvian characteristics, He selected those races of the created kinds which were best suited to the more difficult postdiluvian period, and these were preserved in the ark. We occasionally find people who worry about how Noah could house in his ark such ponderous dinosaur forms as the fifty-ton plant-eating *Brachiosaurus*, the eighty-foot vegetarian *Diplodocus*, and horrible nineteen-foot high *Tyrannosaurus*. But it is reasonable to assume that all the members of these races of large dinosaurs perished in the flood. Man still had a destiny before him, and God knew that he could not compete with such colossal forms. The dinosaur *baramins* were doubtless preserved in some of their smaller races such as the ostrich dinosaur, *Stuthiomimus*, and *Compsognathus*, which was no larger than a chicken." [The name *baramin* (plural *baramins*) for the created unit … this word is formed from the two Hebrew roots, *bara*, "to create," and *min*, "kind." – Marsh]

Life, Man, and Time

P.156

Marsh gives further clarification:

"But we must keep in mind that God could look ahead and see that man was going to continue sinful and that one thing to be accomplished by this flood was the preparation of an earth better suited to a sinful man who would diminish in size and strength. There can be no question that dinosaurs were represented, possibly by forms like *Compsognathus*, which was no larger than a rooster. But we would expect the terrible flesh-eating *Tyrannosaurus* to be left outside, along with the vegetarian but tremendously ungainly fellow reptiles, *Diplodocus* and *Brontosaurus*, whose very bulky, thirty-five and fifty tons respectively, would make them a hazard around the houses of postdiluvian man."

[Ibid. P.106]

Marsh claims dinosaurs were taken into Noah's Ark at the time of the Great Flood but he makes it clear that carnivores (flesh eaters) and large dinosaurs (sauropods) were left out. This differs from the other creationists, who have written the above juvenile books. They insist every KIND of dinosaur, without exception, had to be on the ark in order to comply with the meaning of Genesis 6:19. Marsh says that dinosaur kinds were taken into the ark with the exception of the meat eaters and huge dinosaurs. He maintains this thought is still in keeping with Genesis 6:19 since dinosaurs were represented as *kinds of land animals*.

Whatever the above mentioned authors meant by kinds or types of dinosaurs and implied "species," the fact remains, Marsh does not give sauropods or certain flesh eaters, a boarding pass for the Ark, while the other authors did. Most of ICS creationists believe that sauropods lived past the flood and right on up to the time of Job. A few or all believe that *Mokele-Mbembe* (a sauropod) is quite possibly living today in the Congo. This makes no sense to me and to believe that God took the types of meat eaters on board the Ark such as *Dromaeosaurids*, *Carnosaurs*, and *Tyrannosaurids*, is completely implausible to my way of thinking.

I have one more quote from another juvenile book written by Ruth Wheeler and Harold G. Coffin:

"Although many kinds of animals went into the ark, none of the dinosaurs did. God saw that Satan had tampered with his creatures. He did not save in the ark animals that were not like those He had first created. After the flood, people became smaller and weaker over the generations. So God did not save the animals that were too big and dangerous for the people after the flood to control. He allowed the dinosaurs to be destroyed by the flood."

Dinosaurs (A juvenile book)

P.24

This new idea is unlike any theory that we have read so far; none of the dinosaurs were taken into the Ark. In summary, the above creationists have one of three beliefs:

*All dinosaurs were taken into the Ark. That is, representatives of all kinds either in the form of eggs or juveniles. This would include meat eaters and sauropods.

*Dinosaurs were taken into the Ark with the exceptions of carnivores and sauropods.

*No dinosaurs were taken into the Ark. [Special Note: With this concept, I suppose the authors would not think that they had overlooked Genesis 6:19 since they had already stipulated that the dinosaur kingdoms was tampered with by Satan and was no longer like God's original creation]

I will now state my opinion. On the one hand, most of the dinosaur kind (as well as all other kinds of land animals) was taken into the Ark. I base this position on Genesis 6:19-20; 7:15-16. On the other hand, I find it impossible to believe that God would take on the Ark the major types of bloodthirsty species of carnivorous dinosaurs. I see them as possible genetic misfits caused and brought about through the work of Satan who constantly seeks to disparage the Creator of love and goodness. The prince of evil has poured blood over the beautiful canvass of nature, to ruin God's perfect artistry of animals, to change man's view of God from that of a loving and merciful progenitor to that of a tyrant who feeds on hatred and violence.

Surely, the dinosaur kind was represented on the Ark to keep harmony with God's command in Genesis 6:19-20 and Genesis 7:15-16. But the dinosaur types represented, of course, would include the non-violent, the small, and the more docile. The ferocious killers were kept from boarding the ark. Also, I believe and go along with Marsh, sauropods or large dinosaurs were kept off the Ark. I realize that this conviction, in turn, can lead to the interpretive difficulty with the 40th chapter of the book of Job since *Job describes a sauropod* about 1500 years before the birth of Christ and almost 150 years after the Ice Age. Rather than give a preview of my answers to this so-called dilemma, I will refer my readers to QUESTIONS SIXTEEN AND SEVENTEEN: What is the *Behemoth* in the book of Job, chapter 40? Did Job actually see a dinosaur in his day?

AFTER THE FLOOD

QUESTION SIX:

IS THE ACCOUNT OF MAN'S FOOTPRINTS DISCOVERED WITH DINOSAUR TRACK WAYS AT THE PALUXY RIVER NEAR GLEN ROSE TEXAS, A RELIABLE ACCOUNT?

ANSWER:

[This question I have pondered for many years and is personally made up for this book. After all, I had questions, which needed to be answered. I express my gratitude to those writers who, through their personal research in the field, settled the issue for me. I will relay to you what I have learned from them]

Let me lead my readers through a short but detailed history as to why I remain skeptical of the events that took place near Glen Rose, Texas:

In May 1939, Roland T. Bird of the Department of Vertebrate Paleontology, the American Museum of Natural History, discovered fine clean tracks of the dinosaurs, *Brontosaurus* and *Tyrannosaurus* in the Paluxy Riverbed near Glen Rose, Texas. These beautifully preserved tracks were, according to deep time geologists, 140 million years old. Later, Bird also examined certain stones, containing human footprints, which were allegedly cut from the same riverbed and the same geological formation. So far, this is the way the account is recorded in most of the books and reports dealing with the issue of Bird's discovery.

[Pittack - As we shall soon find out, some creationists are quick to pick up on the account that the tracks of man and dinosaurs were contemporaneous but these same creationists have been negligent in reporting **all the facts** of Bird's descriptions and especially the important **field research** that has been done by **other creation-scientists** at the Paluxy River. They have also been remiss in their keeping *two events* completely separated – the discovery of dinosaur trackways **IN THE FIELD** and the examination of human footprints **OUT OF THE FIELD**. *The account of contemporaneous footprints, held by some creationists, is only one version of the story*]

Dr. Bird gives the following report:

"For a moment I had them [the stones] to myself, - the strangest thing of their kind I had ever seen. On the surface of each was splayed the near-likeness of a human foot, *perfect in every anatomical detail*. But each imprint was 15 inches long. *When I heard there were dinosaur tracks in exactly the same type of stone from apparently and identical stratigraphic level, my thoroughly revived curiosity could scarcely be contained. Even the possibility of such an association seemed incredible. Both types came from Glen Rose.*" [Italics, Bird]

[Roland T. Bird, *Natural History*, May 1939, Pp.255-56. Quoted in "Man's Origin, Man's Destiny" by A.E. Wilder-Smith, p.137]

From this report, Bird says, "I had them [the stones] to myself ..." I would urge my readers to make a note that **Bird had the stones!** What does this mean specifically? It denotes that **Bird did not actually see these footprints first-hand at the riverbed.** They had already been *allegedly* cut out from the bed of the Paluxy River. Bird had photographs of these stones made for his article and assumed that the human footprints were false. Note that Bird "*heard* there were dinosaur tracks in exactly the same type of stone." To me, this does not sound like first-hand data. Rather, it sounds like word of mouth information. And the stones, **since they were not seen in situ**, could in no way be classified as direct evidence of authentic phenomena. Bird was more than correct in his evaluation of the human footprints (in assuming they were false) in spite of what some creationists thought back in the 1930s or what other creationists think in this present-day.

Richard M. Ritland (a creation-scientist), who in 1970 was Director of the Geoscience Research Institute, wrote the book, *A Search for Meaning in Nature* [A New Look at Creation and Evolution]

Ritland comments on Bird's report:

"Accounts of giant human footprints reportedly observed along the Paluxy River a few miles from Glen Rose, Texas, have received far-reaching publicity. These tracks were reported in a popular magazine article on dinosaur track hunting by Roland T. Bird of the American Museum. ***Bird never saw any clear-cut 'human-like tracks' in the rock strata along the river except for ill-defined impressions which lacked sufficient details on which to base conclusions.*** However, at an Indian trading post in New Mexico he had seen 'human-like' tracks about fifteen inches long as well as dinosaur tracks. These were *reportedly* from the Paluxy, and preserved such perfect detail that he suspected 'the entire lot has been fashioned by some stone artist.'" [Emphasis mine]

P.230

I have read accounts written by creationists, who are quick to criticize Bird for his "awkward observations" and "scientific circles" and for his claiming that the man tracks or the dinosaur tracks must have been falsified. I can understand where my fellow-creationists are coming from. They figure that Bird and his scientific cohorts had avoided the problem of dinosaurs and man being contemporaneous and its implication that the "whole structure of Darwinism" would be overturned if such a geological event proved true.

A.E. Wilder-Smith writes his **opinion** of Dr. Bird's evaluation of the tracks which, I believe, is **entirely inaccurate**:

"Dr. Bird reproduces a photograph of the man tracks in his article mentioned. But except for saying that they were probably falsified, *for which assumption there is not the slightest evidence,* the matter is left unsolved." [Italics, mine]

Man's Origin, Man's Destiny

P.137

And Whitcomb and Morris [**Pittack** - Agreeing with Wilder-Smith in inaccuracy], **confusing fieldwork with non-field work**, write:

"Geologists have rejected this evidence [**Pittack** - **What evidence?**], preferring to believe that the human footprints were created by some modern artist [**Pittack** - **For which there is plenty of evidence**], while at the same time accepting the dinosaur prints as genuine. If anything, the dinosaur prints look more 'artificial' than the human, but the genuineness of neither would be questioned at all was it not for the geologically sacrosanct evolutionary time-scale."

The Genesis Flood

P.174

[**Pittack** - I love to read the copious writings of Whitcomb and Morris! These men are truly great scholars and they wrote as if their lives were in the balance. However, the above statement sets me to wondering if these two men actually investigated the facts through field work or if they simply sat around as armchair detectives]

The above two quotes from the three creationists are partially correct but only up to a certain point. They are correct in their assumption that evolutionary postulates could not possibly accept the contemporaneous existence of man with dinosaurs. Such acceptance would nullify the evolutionary belief of man's late existence and his descent from primates.

On the other hand, who would blame Bird for judging the footprints to be of uncertain validity? *He actually saw the genuine dinosaur track ways but he only heard about the numerous farmers' stories describing the giant human tracks found at the Paluxy River and evidenced only in the stones, which were purportedly cut from the river.* Again, I would urge my readers to take note that the alleged giant human footprints, which are supposed to overlap the dinosaur footprints, look nothing like the photos taken by C.L. Burdick. Those "human foot prints" allegedly cut out from the bed of the Paluxy River, actually – in situ – appear as *random erosional markings* (Ritland). The photographs taken by Burdick were said to have been the *stones cut out from the Paluxy River*. These photographs appear in *The Genesis Flood* by Whitcomb and Morris, pages 174,175. But the footprints are too perfect and, in fact, so *perfect*, they appeared false to Bird. Ritland reports the "perfect" feet as to good to be true. Sure enough! "[There was] **one too many friction pads on each toe**. Either these tracks do not match human feet perfectly or else the stone artist failed in the detail. While this story may have some basis in fact, the details are clouded and questionable." *(A Search for Meaning in Nature* by Richard M. Ritland, P.232) [Italics, mine]

Over periods of time, giant human footprints have been purchased from merchants, creationists have also heard more reports from farmers, numerous dinosaur tracks have been discovered along the Paluxy River "but none of the 'man tracks' have ever been authenticated" (Ritland).

Whitcomb and Morris have this to say about Bird's original comments of May 1939:

"Bird described in detail the remarkable foot-prints in the Cretaceous strata of central Texas in the Paluxy River bed. It is amazing the way he dismisses the giant human foot-prints found there as either fakes or as made by some as yet unknown animal, while reporting so enthusiastically of the dinosaur foot-prints found in the same stratum. The human foot-prints admittedly looked genuine and there was no evidence as to who the 'artist' might have been [**Pittack** - There is, in fact, **overwhelming evidence** discovered by Ritland in his visit to Glen Rose] but Bird summarily rejected their evidence on the basis of the fact that it is known that humans were not living in the Cretaceous!"

The Genesis Flood

P.174

The above quote is filled with so many inaccuracies, it is difficult for me to comment but I will make an attempt to derive as much sense out of it as is possible... ... ...

"It is amazing" Whitcomb and Morris write. But *not so amazing* when you know Bird actually examined the dinosaur track ways in the Cretaceous strata but saw merely what appeared to be cut outs of stones containing human foot-prints that were *allegedly taken from the same strata*. Bird did not, in fact, know for a certainty that these giant human prints were *taken from the same strata* since they were *not seen "in situ."*

In December of 1958, Richard M. Ritland, a Seventh-day Adventist creationist, visited the Glen Rose – Paluxy River area and this is his report:

"I inquired of a number of the old-time residents regarding the footprint stories. A local businessman and long-time resident, who happened to have two chiseled-out replicas of dinosaur tracks for sale, told me that the person from whom he had obtained these tracks ... **had made and sold many such footprints chiefly to curio dealers**. On locating this man who lived in a very humble dwelling on the edge of the village, I found him congenial but **rather guarded**. He must have conjectured that I was there to check on the authenticity of 'fossil' tracks he may have **suspected** I had purchased as 'genuine' but later questioned.

At first he firmly stated that he had never carved out or sold any footprints. After visiting awhile he warmed up to the subject and **assured me that if he had ever chiseled out any footprints they would be a lot better quality than those I had seen at the Glen Rose merchant's.** He took me around behind his house and said, 'Here, **I'll give you one.**' Although he denied having made any human tracks, another resident said he understood that the old gentleman had chiseled out some on the river bank years before."** [Italics, mine]

A Search for Meaning in Nature

Richard M. Ritland

P.232

As I view the **entire order of events** and what has been said about the Paluxy River discovery, I remain totally skeptical regarding the human footprints. Way back in 1958, Richard M. Ritland (a Christian paleontologist) discovered on his visit to Glen Rose – Paluxy River area, numerous conflicting details. After reading *The Genesis Flood* at the age of twenty-five, I had my doubts about the authenticity of the human footprints, even though I was a creationist. At the age of thirty-six I read *A Search for Meaning in Nature* by Ritland and had my reservations confirmed as true.

The clincher that led me to the absolute conviction the human footprints were false, was my reading of *Creation and Evolution* by Alan Hayward in the year 1985. At the time, I was forty-nine. In a moment I will tell you why Hayward had convinced me the human footprints should be questioned. I can assure my readers that no one believes more than I; man lived right along the side of dinosaurs. That is, they were contemporaneous. I think that my responses to the questions in this book establish that fact beyond any question.

But as much as I would like to believe the story of giant human footprints at the Paluxy River bed, I am one of those creationists that have repudiated the Paluxy claim. I can't help but feel: when my fellow creationists, with their tending to offer the alleged find at Paluxy, as a proof against the long ages separating dinosaurs from man, it turns evolutionists and others away from looking at the many truths creationists print in their books.

What turned me off when reading about the human footprints at the age of twenty-five; not only were the footprints said to be human but they were supposed to be "giant" human, footprints. I believe in the giants mentioned in the Bible but to believe that this "rare" discovery just happened to be "giant" footprints along with dinosaur track ways was too much for me to accept. If anything, it aroused my suspicions.

I would like to point out what two creationists have published about the human footprints. Alan Hayward mentions Christopher Weber and Laurie Godfrey in Creation and Evolution. He gives a summary of their **findings**. You don't discover these **findings** in any recent books on creationism. [**Pittack** - I suppose that orthodox creationist writers do not bother with Hayward, since he at times, holds to radical viewpoints]. Since the **findings** are either not known by present-day creationists or if they are known, some creationists prefer not to believe them. But in so doing, they are refuting the **findings of their very own allies**, who believe in God and hold to the essential views on creationism. These creationist scientists (Weber and Godfrey) have taken time to investigate further into the subject of the track ways and footprints. They have by-passed the blocks that were allegedly cut from the riverbed, the reports of farmers, and the second-hand information provided by laymen and villagers who swear to the footprints authenticity. After examining the Paluxy River phenomena "in situ" the following summary is based on the conclusions of their investigation. I will share only the first five points of their **findings**:

(1) It is well known that there was a carnivorous dinosaur with three toes. Depending upon how it moved its feet, and how well the impressions were preserved, the tracks it left behind sometimes look quite like human footprints.

(2) The Paluxy footprints are too far apart to have been made by humans, even long-legged giants. But they do fit the known stride of the three-toed dinosaur.

(3) Sometimes, if you follow along the line of the 'human' footprints, the tracks continue as well-defined three-toed dinosaur tracks.

(4) Some of the 'human' tracks have clear signs of a claw projecting from the 'heel'.

(5) They quote the geologist Berney Neufeld, who is a Seventh - day Adventist and a creationist. He has made a detailed study of the Paluxy tracks, and has published his conclusions. Some of the "footprints" are random erosional markings, he says, and the three-toed dinosaur made the rest.

(The **findings** of Christopher Weber and Laurie Godfrey appear in *Creation and Evolution* by Alan Hayward, P.149)

Remember! The so-called human footprints, seen in situ, are nothing like the photograph in the *The Genesis Flood* (written by Whitcomb and Morris) and appearing on pages 174, 175. The photograph of the human footprints is close to perfect but the footprints were not seen in the riverbed. It was only said the footprints were *cut out from the riverbed*. No person but God Himself, really knows if this fact is the truth and, therefore, authentic phenomenon. The "human" footprints, that were seen in situ by Berney Neufeld, he described as "random erosional markings." This description is a far cry from the photograph, which appears on pages 174-175 in *The Genesis Flood* and pictures almost PERFECT FEET. Roland T. Bird, as an evolutionist, did not believe that dinosaurs lived contemporaneously with man. This was his main reason for doubting the human footprints. However, as a creationist, who does believe that man and dinosaurs lived together, I cannot accept the human footprints simply because they were not found in situ at the Paluxy River bed. I have good reason for my doubting, which have been indicated in the above events, which took place near Glen Rose, Texas. Also, Ritland – a Seventh-day Adventist creationist – discovered that the human footprints had "one too many friction pads on each toe" and the man tracks had never "been authenticated" (See page 30 in this book).

This is one issue I fear will never be settled among creationists since there will always be those who fail to see the evidence against the Paluxy discoveries. I am fully persuaded we ought to be thankful for such investigations by the above fellow creationists that have been mentioned and welcome their assessments although their findings may undermine the long-held and long-cherished beliefs about the Paluxy, giant, human footprints. On the one hand, I write to advance the cause of creationism since I know it to be true. On the other hand, I will advance the cause of creationists only as they continue to operate within the realm of valid facts and reasonable assessments, based on available evidence.

For those creationists who wonder about my skepticism; I also wonder about those of you who think that gullibility is an attribute to be coveted and being suspicious is a trait to be spurned. Before I buy into anything, which has to do with the upholding of creationism; I want to make certain that gathered facts are really facts that can make me feel comfortable in my thinking. In conclusion, *there are simply too many loopholes in the account of human footprints having been found with dinosaur tracks at Paluxy for it to be a reliable account*. I am among those creationists who not only repudiate it but remain embarrassed to know that the story still stands and is being circulated as a standard argument for a young earth. In talking to some creationists, the thoughts of the Paluxy River dinosaur trackways and man's footprints being contemporaneous, I gather, **is some sacred reflection enshrined within their thoughts**.

QUESTION SEVEN:

WHERE ARE DINOSAUR GRAVEYARDS OR QUARRIES LOCATED ON THIS EARTH?

ANSWER:

[The night this question was posited, I mentioned a few graveyards discovered in the United States and some others found in additional parts of the world. This question came in by way of a hand-microphone. I presently refer the reader to examples of these same graveyards in QUESTION THIRTY-SIX and the section entitled "Paleontology – Dinosaur Graveyards." For more specific details of certain graveyards, the reader is referred to Pittack's book, *The Archaeopteryx Controversy*, chapter 12, Section (2) Dinosaur Graveyards]

QUESTION EIGHT:

WHEN THE DINOSAURS DIED, DID THE SUBSTANCE FROM THE DECOMPOSITION GO INTO THE MAKING OF PETROLEUM AND THE EXISTANCE OF PETROLEUM?

ANSWER:

[Many questions placed in the DINOSAUR QUESTION BOX, I rated as fair to excellent. This is an excellent question that I answered by way of the hand-microphone]

This is an excellent question and it has to do with a branch of economic geology called petroleum geology. A petroleum geologist is involved in the exploration of oil and gas accumulations in the earth and is concerned with the problem of finding hydrocarbons.

A hydrocarbon is any organic compound (gas, liquid, or solid) consisting solely of carbon and hydrogen. And, of course, our mind immediately causes us to think of coal and oil.

Earth's fossil fuels, coal, and oil were formed from accumulated organic material buried by the Flood. I am not adept in the knowledge of the various theories of inorganic and organic origin of petroleum but as far as I do know, petroleum is best judged to be *organic in origin.*

The vast reservoirs of the organic remains of plant and animals are a primary source of petroleum. In that vast herds of dinosaurs perished in the Flood, I can only assume that many of them, the decomposition of their bodies contributed to petroleum accumulations.

[Special Note on Genesis 6:14 for my readers: Asphalt is a dark brown to black viscous liquid consisting almost entirely of carbon and hydrogen. *This substance is also known as pitch.* In Genesis 6:14, Noah was instructed to build an Ark, 450 feet long, 75 feet wide and 45 feet high. God told Noah to "coat it with pitch inside and out." This, of course, would make the ark watertight and showed *the availability of pitch before the Flood.* This *pitch* must have been *sapropel,* which could have been produced in the 1,656 years before the Flood. According to Woodmorappe, sapropel is jellylike ooze or sludge composed most often of putrefying algae in an anaerobic environment. It is found on the shallow bottoms of lakes and seas and may be a source material for petroleum]

QUESTION NINE:

DINOSAURS ARE BURIED IN THE GROUND. HOW DO WE KNOW THE BIBLE FLOOD AND NOT JUST DIFFERENT FLOODS THROUGHOUT TIME, BURIED THEM?

ANSWER:

[This question came in through the hand-microphone]

Some dinosaurs were buried by local flooding just as animals die today in local floods. This is the short answer.

On the other hand, there are vast graveyards of buried dinosaurs throughout the earth. These graveyards, filled with dinosaur bones, can be accounted for only on the basis of the biblical Flood. The dinosaur graveyards attest to quick burial. There had to be rapid burial in order for the dinosaur bones to be preserved. Most creationists believe that the Universal Flood destroyed the main body of the dinosaur kingdoms. This seems to be the only answer to the great mystery of dinosaur extinction. The dinosaur graveyards seem to be enough evidence for establishing a Universal Flood. The following facts will serve as sufficient examples:

*At the Dinosaur National Monument there are countless thousands of bones all jumbled together. The Great Flood waters stand out as the only possible explanation for such a burial.

*There is an Allosaurus graveyard with evidence of mass destruction; over 10,000 Allosaurus bones in the same area in Utah.

*There is a quarry in West Germany containing thousands of Plateosaurus bones; * the rich bone beds in Mongolia contain many different species of dinosaurs, and *the famous bone-yards in Africa contain many thousands of dinosaur bones.

All these graveyards and many more that could be mentioned constitute convincing evidence for the biblical Flood. [The readers are referred to QUESTION 36 and the section entitled, "Paleontology – Dinosaur Graveyards."]

QUESTION TEN:

THE GRAVEYARDS ARE FAIRLY GOOD EVIDENCE FOR A UNIVERSAL FLOOD BUT IS THERE ANY SOLID OR MORE CONVINCING EVIDENCE THAT A UNIVERSAL FLOOD IS RESPONSIBLE FOR THE EARTH'S FORMATIONS IN WHICH MOST DINOSAUR FOSSILS AND OTHER FOSSILIZED ANIMALS ARE FOUND?

ANSWER:

[This is another anticipated question covered in one of my lectures]

There are convincing evidences for a Universal Flood, which can readily be observed in the geological strata. If there was a biblical Flood, then there should be evidences. If there was a Great Catastrophe that inundated the earth by water, then much evidence should remain.

In the geological record there are many indications of a major flooding of the world by water. In California, our home-state, one needs to go on a geological trip only to such places as Vasquez Rocks or the Devil's Punch Bowl to see evidences for extensive water action and catastrophism that support the Genesis account of the Flood. Catastrophic action is seen throughout the world.

Sedimentary deposits constitute about 75% of the rocks exposed on the earth. Dinosaurs are buried in such sedimentary type rock. The following examples should make us aware why sediments serve as vast graveyards for the entombment and preservation of dinosaurs and other animals:

*There are great quantities of water and wind deposited sedimentary rock throughout the entire earth. The deposits are extremely deep and geologists cannot determine their source. Uniformity is unable to explain the deposits because gradual submergence and slow accumulations of sediments by erosion cannot account for the vast quantities of sedimentary materials.

* Sediments irrespective of the height or extent of adjacent landscapes have filled large depressions on this earth. Only a World Wide Flood could have made this possible.

*In North America, there are great beds of sandstone and one of which is 500 feet thick. Beds of sandstone are not forming anyplace in the world today. Flowing rivers or streams could not have produced these extensive sand beds. Uniformity is not the explanation. But the Noachian Flood is the answer to these unusual phenomena.

*The Northern Rockies show exposures of more than 4,000 feet of sedimentary strata. The evidence shows they have been deposited rapidly. Delicate fossils have been preserved in excellent condition. The burial of vast numbers of Trilobites and other invertebrates frequently show no sign of decay or disintegration.

These are proofs that the sediments did not form by a process of gradual accumulation over millions of years.

In conclusion: the earth's strata cannot be in harmony with the belief that their accumulations took millions of years to form. Rather, the Great or World Wide Flood called the Noachian Flood deposited the strata quickly. The Bible states, "Speak to the earth and it will teach thee." The earth does not teach its strata indicate a time period going backward in time 4 ½ billion years; its does not teach the Doctrine of Uniformitarianism. The earth does teach it is a young earth, geologically speaking; its physical records constitute a clear picture of the Catastrophic Forces, which shaped it.

QUESTION ELEVEN:

THE OLD TESTAMENT OF THE BIBLE SEEMS TO SAY THAT THE GREAT FLOOD WAS UNIVERSAL AND NOT LOCAL. BUT I BELIEVE THE GENESIS STORY OF THE FLOOD IS A MYTH AND HAS NO HISTORICAL BASIS. IS THERE ANYTHING IN THE NEW TESTAMENT THAT WOULD MAKE IT CLEAR THE FLOOD WAS REAL HISTORY AND NOT A MADE UP STORY?

ANSWER:

[Someone who had turned it in to THE DINOSAUR QUESTION BOX posed the question. The answer I gave was a shortened version compared to the following words, which are for my readers]

Actually, there is an immense amount of biblical evidence attesting to the Flood as being a part of this earth's history. Since the formulator of the question seems to doubt the Old Testament, it can be assumed that this person has more confidence in the New Testament. [The establishment of the Old Testament was the only inspired or "God breathed" source of information that was available to Christ and the apostles and became the source of their preaching throughout the early and middle part of the first century. The Old Testament is a man-made term but nevertheless the 39 books was the Inspired Word of God made known through the prophets of old. But being old, as far as time is concerned, does not invalidate the Special Revelation of God nor deny the Truthfulness of His Message] For now and for the sake of the person who posits the question, the New Testament will be consulted in order to answer the question under consideration. You will notice how the New Testament spokesmen in no way contradict the Old Testament account of Noah's Flood and its World Wide scope.

To begin with, the Flood is well covered in the book of Genesis. Moses is credited with writing Genesis since it is part of the Pentateuch. The question that must be asked – Does the New Testament support the writings of Moses in the book of Genesis? Is there an indication that his account of the Flood was anything else than true and actual history?

Jesus had this to say in John 5:46-47:

"For had ye believed Moses, ye would have believed me: for he wrote of me. But if ye believe not his writings, how shall ye believe my words?"

What were the writings of Moses? – The book of Job and the Pentateuch. The Pentateuch consists of five books: Genesis, Exodus, Leviticus, Numbers, and Deuteronomy. Moses, in fact, wrote in the book of Genesis about Noah, the preparing of the ark, and the Great Flood that destroyed the world.

Jesus, in turn, took up the historical theme of Moses concerning the Flood. **Matthew** has recorded the words of Christ **(24:37-39):**

"But as the days of Noe were, so shall also the coming of the Son of Man be. For as in the days that were before the flood they were eating and drinking, marrying and giving in marriage, until the day that Noe entered the ark. And knew not until the flood came, and took them all away; so shall also the coming of the Son of man be."

Christ, in this passage, was comparing the reality of His second coming to the reality of an historical event in the days of Noah. Just as individuals were not prepared for the destruction of the world that came by the Flood of the past, so many individuals will not be prepared for the destruction that will come in the future at Christ's second coming.

Jesus, without question, accepted the account of the Flood in Genesis as *true and authentic history. He never intimated that the flood narrative was mythological.* Otherwise, His powerful words concerning His second coming would have *lost their force* if such an event were compared to a myth. Jesus, most assuredly, believed in a World- Wide Flood. All, who are followers of Christ, should accept the fact of the Flood account in the book of the Genesis chronicle, as being true and valid history.

The apostle Paul also believed in the Flood as an historical event. He wrote in **Hebrews 11:7:**

"By faith Noah, being warned of God of things not seen as yet, moved with fear, prepared an ark to the saving of his house; by which he condemned the world, and became heir of righteousness which is by faith."

Noah was commanded by God to build an ark and he did so. Many years later, Noah's faith and obedience were honored in Paul's epistle to the Hebrews. There is not the slightest hint that the building of an ark, in preparation for the Great Flood, was not an historical event. The eleventh chapter of Hebrews portrays a number of men and women who "all died in the faith" and served as an inspiration to the readers of Paul's epistle. They were historical figures who "obtained a good report" from God. If these were mythological people, then the chapter would hardly serve the purpose for which it was intended.

The apostle Peter makes no less than three comments concerning the Noachian Flood. In **I Peter 3:20**, Peter speaks of God waiting in the days of Noah. That is, God waiting 120 years for mankind to respond to Noah's preaching. Also, the preparation of the ark is mentioned and the saving of eight souls from the flood. The eight souls that were saved included Noah, his three sons, and the four wives. **If the account of the Flood in Genesis were mythological, then Peter would not have regarded the account as history. Peter had every intention of communicating to his readers the authenticity of the Flood event and that is exactly what he did.** [Note: During the 120 years of Noah's preaching, we can assume or at least hope that many individuals responded to his message before their death. The 120 years not only established that God is long-suffering and not willing that any should perish but it gave the inhabitants of the then known world, plenty of time to find out, by word of mouth, the account of that strange preacher who stood before a tremendous vessel (in the process of being built) and delivered earnest and inspiring sermons. Some of those people, who lived far and wide on the face of the earth, were lead by the Spirit of God to travel long distances to hear the call to repentance and salvation. **It matters not that people did not live in the remotest part of the globe. The entire world was to be inundated and made anew just as the world, in the last days, will be purged with fire and made anew for the redeemed of God]**

Another reference from Peter is found in his second epistle, **II Peter 2:5:**

"And spared not the old world, but saved Noah the eighth person [Noah's wife, his three sons and their wives, and Noah], a preacher of righteousness, bringing in the flood upon the world of the ungodly."

It is impossible to view these words outside of an historical context. Peter wrote of a ***real person*** named Noah who preached ***real sermons*** to ***real people***. Noah was saved from a ***real Flood*** that brought ***real destruction*** upon ***real sinners*** who would not repent. There is no indication that the Flood of Noah's day was anything but ***real history***.

One more passage from the pen of Peter, **II Peter 3:3-7:**

"Knowing this first, that there shall come in the last days scoffers, walking after their own lusts,

And saying, where is the promise of his coming? For since the fathers fell asleep, all things continue as they were from the beginning of creation.

For this they are willingly are ignorant of, that by the word of God the heavens were of old, and the earth standing out of the water and in the water:

Whereby the world that then was, being overflowed with water, perished:

But the heavens and the earth which are now, by the same word are kept in store, reserved unto fire against the Day of Judgment and perdition of ungodly men."

What words could Peter have used to better describe historical events? He speaks of scoffers who doubted the flood event and other scoffers who doubt the second coming of Jesus. **If the flood of Noah's day were only a myth, then Peter would not have made an issue of men being scoffers of the event. Vividly, Peter writes of things he believed were true. He writes of:**

*Scoffers who did not believe in the Flood.

*The Flood coming upon the earth by God's word.

*The complete and total inundation of the world.

*The Universality of the Flood.

*An historical judgment upon mankind by a Flood that caused them to perish.

*A future judgment by fire upon ungodly men.

The words are powerful and potent. To view the language of the apostle as anything less than historical when it comes to the Flood and events surrounding it, is to do violence to the original Greek language and the modern languages that translates the Scriptural passages.

Jesus spoke about the Noachian Flood and Paul and Peter wrote about it. The Bible passages cited above demonstrate very clearly the Flood was real history and not a fictitious story. The three great biblical personages did not believe the Flood to be mythological. They accepted the Genesis account of water overflowing the earth as true and reliable history. There is nothing in their words or writings to indicate otherwise. **Devil's Punch Bowl, Red Rock Canyon, and Vasquez Rocks** are areas in our home state of southern California. **If Jesus, Paul, and Peter were to stand at these regions of geology and nature, they would all agree that the Noachian Flood and not the result of uniformity caused the formations.** *And that would be due to their common belief in the historicity of the Universal Flood.*

DINOSAURS AND MAN

QUESTION TWELVE:

SINCE ADAM AND EVE WERE 18 FEET TALL, WOULDN'T ALL THE ANIMALS HAVE BEEN PROPORTIONAL IN THEIR TALLNESS TO OUR FIRST PARENTS, THAN THEY ARE NOW?

ANSWER:

[This question rather surprised me. It came from the QUESTION BOX and was one of those types that required some extra thought. I had never before seen a question quite like this one]

Although the fossil record indicates that some animals and some plants were larger than similar species of animals and plants today, I don't believe that God had proportion in mind when he created the animals for man. Although I agree that (due to his perfection, prior to sin) Adam's height was probably greater than that of men who presently live on the earth, I am uncertain about the given height of 18 feet in your question. But if dinosaurs were truly in proportion to Adam, then why were some dinosaurs no bigger than a bird (*Microraptor* – "Tiny Thief") and some dinosaurs were over 100 feet long (*Supersaurus* – "Super Lizard") to a 150 long (Breviparopus).

I have pointed out that the dinosaur "models" came in all shapes and sizes. Your question infers that you believe that the large size of the dinosaurs made them different from the animals of today but *large size was not characteristic of all dinosaurs.*

The name "dinosaur" came from British scientist Sir Richard Owen (a creationist) in 1872. The meaning of "dinosaur" is "terrible lizard" and this has popularized the idea that dinosaurs were all gigantic savage monsters. This is far from the truth. Had Owen known about the *smaller* dinosaurs, *he may never have coined the word dinosaur.*

The dinosaurs, in many ways, were similar to other animals but *they did have several features that were not shared with other animals*: [The list of features is made up by Don Lessem]

  *They had three vertebrae in the sacrum area;

  *A thigh bone held straight beneath the body;

  *A twisted shin bone;

  *A bird-like foot; and

  *a very small forth finger of the hand.

Also, Dinosaurs were divided into two groups by their hip structure. We are out of answer time and so I will simply mention the *bird-hipped* and *lizard-hipped* dinosaurs. A few final words: no earth animal has reached the enormous size of the sauropod dinosaur.

This particular creation alerts me to the fact: proportion was not in the plans of God but rather to make an impact on man with His power as Creator.

[For the above characteristics, which dinosaurs do not share with other animals, I would refer my readers to *Time for Learning Dinosaurs* written by Don Lessem, P.11]

QUESTION THIRTEEN:

WHAT ARE THE LEGENDS AND STORIES OF DRAGONS IN EUROPEAN AND CHINESE LORE AND LITERATURE IF NOT A TRIBAL MEMORY OF DINOSAURS?

ANSWER:

[I was happy to see this question in the DINOSAUR QUESTION BOX. It gave me the opportunity to say a few things that I probably would have forgotten to bring out to the audience especially concerning "tribal memory"]

This is *an informative question*. The question is really asking if I agree with the idea that the dragon motif, in the legends and stories, can be traced to dinosaurs. Yes, I believe it can. Many of the Chinese still believe dinosaur bones, ground into powder, are a good medicinal agent. *They call the powder "dragon" powder*. This is the *first factor* that leads me to believe Chinese literature and art, which depicts dragons, can be traced back to dinosaurs. The Europeans also have a rich heritage of dragon literature and art, which, no doubt, can also be traced back to dinosaurs. The *second factor* that enables me to equate dragons with dinosaurs is the obvious reality: *many dinosaur species simply look like dragons.*

However, we need to talk about the part of the question that *traces such lore and literature to tribal memories*. If, indeed, the dragon legends are a result of tribal memory, implies individual artists and writers did not have to actually see dinosaurs alive. Certainly, no known civilizations saw any of the original dinosaurs that perished in the Flood. The civilizations did not come into existence until after the Flood and according to chapters 10-11 of Genesis, which outlines *God and the nations*. The people that were alive prior to the Flood were contemporaneous with dinosaurs and, of course, were able to view these creatures.

There were certain representatives of the dinosaur kind, taken into the ark. These dinosaurs did not begin to migrate until 1,657 years after the creation of the world and after being released from the Ark. Michael Oard presents valid reasons for the length of the Ice Age in his outstanding book, *Frozen in Time*. Oard believes and concludes the Ice Age took 500 years to reach its maximum and 200 years to melt. In other words, the Ice Age lasted about 700 years from start to finish. Adding the 700 years to 1657 A.M. brings us to the date, 2,357 A.M. [For the 1657 A.M. determination, the reader is referred back to QUESTION THREE] This A.M. date can be translated to the B.C. date of approximately 1,950 years before the birth of Christ or the time of Abraham. I have been long under the impression, and rightfully so that dinosaurs could not possibly have survived the Ice Age. Therefore, after the time dinosaurs were released from the Ark, the ancestors of the Chinese could have viewed dinosaurs for at least another four centuries and passed on their memory to their progenitors. But these memories were enhanced and proved by the finding of dinosaur bones.

Since Chinese art goes back in time to only about 1,550 B.C. and literature to about 1,400 B.C.; these two forms of culture, therefore, were not the product of any eye-sightings of dinosaurs by the Chinese artists and writers. The imagination that called forth mental dragons, which were depicted in literature and art, was inspired and based upon dinosaur bones that were fully articulated, coupled with the information supplied by Chinese ancestors. The bones that were excavated from the earth were seen *in situ* (in their natural position). When dinosaur bones are found together and not scattered, the formations look like dragons as we know them from art, especially *Styracosaurus* and *Tuojiangosaurus*.

The following statement is apropos to my above observation and is for my readers:

"Could *Tuojiangosaurus* be a dragon? Fossils of two partial skeletons of *Tuojiangosaurus* have been recovered from Szechwan in China, an area rich in dinosaur fossils. Records dating back to AD 265 tell of local villagers collecting these fossils and selling them as dragon bones for use in traditional medicines. With such a long history of fossil collecting in the area, it seems likely that the fossils of *Tuojiangosaurus* were picked up and sold as parts of a mythical ancient dragon."

A Guide to Dinosaurs

Christopher A. Brochu, John Long, Colin McHenry, John D. Scanlon, Paul Willis

Consultant editor – Michael K. Brett-Surman

P.145

To conclude, I believe the dragons of legend and literature were products of the imagination based on the bones of dinosaurs, which the Chinese had observed, coupled with information passed on by their ancestors. The Europeans followed over 2,000 years later and as far as they are concerned, either made similar paleontological observations or the dragon motif was assimilated from the Chinese and other cultures.

I take issue with those creationists, who teach that every time a dragon is mentioned in Scripture (the Old and New Testaments), it has reference to a dinosaur. [The readers should refer to QUESTION THIRTY for further clarification]

I also take issue with those creationists, who support the claim that there have been sightings of dinosaurs as late as the 16th century AD. I do believe that dinosaurs lived contemporaneously with man but dinosaurs have been extinct for over 3,600 years – ever since the end of the Ice Age. [More about this issue in QUESTION TWENTY-NINE]

Styracosaurus ("spiked lizard") and *Tuojiangosaurus* ("Tuojiang lizard") are not the only dinosaurs to quicken man's imagination as he fixes on the dragon motif. There are many other restorations and reconstructions of dinosaurs that should convince people of the strong possibilities that ***the idea of dragons came visually from dinosaur excavations.***

The dragon myth employed in art and literature arose through imagination but that imagery was based on the reality of paleotological discoveries or coming upon chance findings; bones exposed by *accidental erosion and fully articulated*. The tribal memory of ancestors was only part of art and literature in the Chinese culture and eventually led to the European cultures.

QUESTION FOURTEEN:

AN ELDER [A LEADER IN THE CHURCH] TOLD ME THIS STORY: MAN MADE THE DINOSAURS A LONG TIME AGO. MAN WAS MUCH MORE INTELLIGENT AT THAT TIME BECAUSE SIN WAS NOT LIKE IT IS NOW. FOR MYSELF, I DON'T BELIEVE THAT MAN MADE DINOSAURS. AM I CORRECT IN MY ASSUMPTION?

ANSWER:

[I considered this to be the most important, philosophical question on dinosaurs that I was called upon to answer from the QUESTION BOX. Since the creator of the question signed his name, I knew the man personally. I spoke with him before the meeting and had an opportunity to get the full meaning of the question. It was not my policy, during any of the meetings, to reveal the source of any inquiry. The person told me that a leader of the church had informed him: Adam and Eve, before sin, created the dinosaurs due to their intelligence. At the meeting, I responded in a direct way without ever revealing the persons name]

Tonight, this question will take up our allotted time of ten minutes for "Answers to Questions." First of all, I am glad you don't believe this story. The story is only that – a story and nothing more. I say this for the following reasons:

*In order for humans to make (create) a dinosaur, they would have to have its DNA. How did Adam and Eve possibly obtain a dinosaur sample?

*If a mere sample of a dinosaur was available, then man would not have the animal's complete genetic code. The DNA for a complete dinosaur would be made up of billions of DNA bases. What would be the good of having a mere sample of a dinosaur?

*For the sake of argument, let us assume that Adam and Eve had the complete system of the genetic code of a dinosaur. How were they enabled, no matter how smart they were, to set up the DNA sequences? Could Adam and Eve afford to purchase a good sequencing machine costing around 150,000 dollars? The cost of sequencing an average size dinosaur would cost around 250 million dollars. Did man have the time, money, and necessary lab equipment to make a dinosaur? I am being facetious but only to reveal the impossibility of making such a creature.

*To fully reconstruct a dinosaur, Adam and Eve would have to have both sets of chromosomes, in all their intricate detail, from each of the dinosaur's parents. Of course, this would be impossible since this particular dinosaur would be the first one created and

49

it would have no parents. How was it possible for Adam and Eve to imagine such an animal in their thought processes to even begin the dinosaur's creation? Adam and Eve, even before sin, did not have the power to create life or any of its forms. Creation was the prerogative of God and God alone.

However, one more example, to further my point, will be given:

*Let us assume that Adam and Eve (along with other mankind such as their sons and daughters – Genesis 5:4) were in possession of the many volumes filled with the genetic code for the creation of a dinosaur. This information would still not be sufficient to accomplish the task of dinosaur making. Why?

Formulate the following picture in your mind:

A present-day car mechanic is in a garage along with others of his crew. They are properly dressed and ready for work. All of them are familiar with the manual that outlines every detail on how to build the latest Mazda. But as they look around the shop, they find that it is empty. They have neither the necessary parts nor the tools for such a construction.

Adam and Eve would have been in a similar position. No matter if they did have the genetic code manuals on how to make a dinosaur; they had neither the necessary parts nor the essential tools. Dear audience! Only God can create. Only He can fill an empty world simply by calling things into existence. With the mere utterance of his voice, he called the dinosaur from the soil and made it into a living creature.

Surely, no man had the power to create but "man made the dinosaurs" seems to imply this very act. "Make" and "create" mean the same thing (Genesis 1:26, 27: Exodus 20:11). Many theologians teach that there are differences between the verbs "create" (bara) and "make" (asah).

[For my readers – I suppose that this is okay as long as we never confuse the issue that "humans can work within that creation and do (asah) things with it, but only God could create (bara) it itself" ("Beginnings and Belongings", page 15, Adult Sabbath School Guide, OCT-NOV-DEC 2006). The Bible makes it clear that God created "all" things and, therefore, *man has created nothing*]

Perhaps, the above story was referring to the intelligence of those people who experiment with genetic factors in bringing about *a new variation of an originally created animal.* In our time, men experiment in genetics. The leg length is made shorter in sheep in order to keep them from jumping fences. But man is not able to create the original gene pools, which made this new variation possible (This is much different from Adam and Eve creating or making the dinosaurs "from scratch").

If variation of dinosaurs is the issue; God brought perfect animals into a perfect world. Adam and Eve were to care for these animals. Why would our first-parents have a desire to make an additional species? God commanded them to care for His created animals and not to try and create a new species through genetic selection. Variation among animal kinds was a part of God's work when He created the original gene pool. There was no need for man to interfere with a process already initiated by God in His original plan. Besides, God had no doubt informed Adam and Eve of His unique plan for variation and the thought of experimentation would not have entered their minds.

It is my conviction that Satan, following sin, brought about the imperfections of the dinosaur kingdoms. He, as some people believe, accomplished this through his knowledge of genetics and by employing hybridization. It is worth mentioning that it would have been impossible for Adam and Eve to create dinosaurs due to this further reason: Only God could have created male and female along with the particular kinds of dinosaurs and having the gene pools necessary for the bringing forth of future varieties.

Before closing, I must mention another story. This account has arisen from the belief of certain creationists: God preserved in the ark every species of animal, which he had created. But the "confused species" which God did not create, resulting from amalgamation, were destroyed in the Flood. The story had been circulated throughout the nineteen century: "amalgamation" means the *sexual union between man and beast that resulted in "monster" forms of life.* I regret to say that some modern creationists actually believe this to be true. In other words, an old belief has been revived.

We should understand that the word *amalgamation,* when talking about animals, is the old term for *hybridization.* Perhaps Satan used the function of hybridization or crossbreeding in the production of change among organisms. He mixed different species of animals that God never intended should be mixed. Over time, certain offspring would be the result of Satan's work that, with his deep knowledge of genetics and biology, brought in life forms far from the original design in God's plan for animal variation. In this sense only, could we say that God did not create these confused species of animals? No small wonder that God warned His people, "Do not mate different kinds of animals." (Leviticus 19:19) On the other hand, we dare not say that Satan or man had the power to create dinosaurs.

The Creator made the original dinosaurs, on the sixth day of creation. Satan, as some people believe, simply altered certain creatures and modified their biological characteristics. That is, certain creatures were altered through hybridization and others were modified by discovering other uses for their claws and teeth. The original instinct of some of the dinosaur families was changed and passed down from parent to offspring through training.

The idea that man was sexually united with beast to produce monstrous life forms is not only scientifically impossible but may turn human thoughts away from true and acceptable science. The things we have talked about tonight will not become a closed issue. But, at the very least, I trust that my fellow Christians will carefully evaluate stories that have to do with the Bible and will refrain from making shallow statements about amalgamation and equating it with the horrendous belief that it has something to do with men's sexual union with beasts and resulting in the production of monster-like, biological forms.

QUESTION FIFTEEN:
A THREE-PART QUESTION

*SCIENTISTS SAY DURING THE TIME OF THE DINOSAURS THERE WAS NO MEN IN EXISTENCE. HOW IS IT THAT THE BEASTS WERE FOUND BUT NOT WITH MEN'S SKELETONS? SCIENTISTS MUST BE RIGHT IN THEIR ASSUMPTION.

ANSWER:

[This series of questions was in the DINOSAUR QUESTION BOX and I decided to present it to the audience on a special night. I often wrote answers on the same sheet on which the questions appeared. The notes helped me to keep in mind certain thoughts, which I planned to present in the future. This is the answer to the first portion of inquiries]

The evolutionist claims that, in evolutionary time, man lived 10 million years ago and the dinosaurs lived 65 to 248 million years ago. The problem for creationists is to falsify the merit of this claim since it seems to be true. If man and the dinosaurs were not separated by long periods of time, then why are their bones not found together? The following is a short version of John Woodmorappe's explanation for such a phenomenon:

1) Generally, human fossils are hard to come by. We find few human remains. There is something about human bones, which hinders their preservation as fossils. Since humans lived away from regions of deposition, their remains are more likely to have rotted away before having any chance to be buried.

2) Humans living near the rivers were not entombed on the flood plains but were flushed out onto the **open** ocean [Pittack - where sea predators devoured them?]

3) As far-fetched as this may appear, fragmentary skeletal remains are erroneously ascribed to some other vertebrate. This frequently happens. It is a general rule: the smaller the fragment the greater the chance of mistaken identity.

4) There is another problem – the intentional non-recognition of human fossils that appear "deep" in the geologic column, where there is the belief that no human remains should be there. Not all evolutionists are honest in the acknowledgement of such discoveries. Often, **such "deep" finds are deliberately ignored, discounted**, or hid from the public. "Forbidden Archaeology" is a must read for those of you who are interested in human origins. If you do not believe that the presence of man existed along the side of the dinosaurs, read the <u>evidence, proving</u> that man lived in the Mesozoic Time (the

Cretaceous, the Jurassic, and the Triassic Eras) corresponding to the <u>great</u> <u>eras</u> <u>of</u> <u>the</u> <u>dinosaur</u> <u>kingdoms</u>. No wonder that evolutionary scientists do not want these hidden facts to be made known to the public! No wonder that Michael Cremo and Richard Thompson entitled their 828-page book, "Forbidden Archaeology" with the subtitle, "The Hidden History of the Human Race!"

5) One more fact for our consideration: "Anthropological studies have shown – perishable buried anthropogenic remains decay completely within *20 years at most*." This means that humans who died before the Flood would not be good candidates for fossilization. [This is because not all ancient environments favored the ultimate preservation of bones. There is simply too much that scientists do not know when it comes to the selectivity of diagenetic conditions for bone preservation; especially when it involves the bones buried deep in the earth. Also, scientists know very little about the chemical conditions that were necessary to preserve bone in palaeoenvironments]

The above five facts are the concepts held by John Woodmorappe in his book *Studies in Flood Geology*, Pp.57-61. The reader is also referred to QUESTION NINETEEN and the *Special Note* at the end of the comments wherein I remind you that there is another excellent reason why human fossils were not preserved.

*DINOSAURS COULDN'T BE A CREATION OF GOD BECAUSE, IF THEY WERE, THEY WOULD HAVE BEEN ON THE ARK. ISN'T IT QUITE OBVIOUS THAT THEIR SIZE WOULD HAVE PREVENTED THEM FROM BEING ON THE ARK?

ANSWER:

[This is the answer to the second portion of inquiries]

The other night, scientific evidence was presented that mankind could not create dinosaurs. Adam and Eve or any other humans, it was noted, did not have the power or necessary means to create dinosaurs. Since I know you are a creationist, I would have you consider two statements by the religious writer, E. G. White.

The first is in *Steps to Christ*, P.67:

"Not all the wisdom and skill of man can produce life in the smallest object of nature. It is only through the life which God Himself has imparted that either plant or animal can live."

The second is in *Patriarchs and Prophets*, P.264:

"The prince of evil, though possessing all the wisdom and might of an angel fallen, has not power to create, or to give life: this is the prerogative of God alone."

I think that we ought to conclude: God, neither man nor Satan, created the dinosaurs (Genesis 1:24-27). Therefore, because the Bible informs us in Genesis 7:2, the basic kinds of land animals were preserved in Noah's ark, we ought to assume this Bible information also included the dinosaur which was unquestionably a land animal.

I will now give you two statements by Frank Lewis Marsh. This creationist gives his observations concerning dinosaurs and Noah's ark. He states that carnivores (flesh-eaters) and large dinosaurs (sauropods) were kept out of the ark. Only the small dinosaurs were granted on-board tickets:

"But there is no reason to believe that *every variety* of antediluvian animal was housed in the Ark. Doubtless all basic types were represented, but we must keep in mind that God could look ahead and see that man was going to continue sinful and that one thing to be accomplished by this Flood was the preparation of an earth better suited to a sinful man who would diminish in size and strength. There can be no question that dinosaurs were represented, possibly by forms like *Compsognathus*, which was no larger than a rooster. But we would expect the terrible flesh-eating *Tyrannosaurus* to be left outside, along with his vegetarian but tremendously ungainly fellow reptiles, *Diplodocus* and *Brontosaurus*, whose very bulk, thirty-five and fifty tons respectively, would make them a hazard around the houses of postdiluvian man." [Italics, author]

Life, Man, and Time

Frank Lewis Marsh

P.106

Marsh writes with further clarification:

"As the Creator looked ahead and saw these postdiluvian characteristics, He selected those races of the created kinds which were best suited to the more difficult postdiluvian period, and these were preserved in the Ark. We occasionally find people who worry about how Noah could house in his Ark such ponderous dinosaur forms as the fifty-ton plant-eating *Brachiosaurus*, the eighty-seven-foot vegetarian *Diplodocus,* and the horrible nineteen-foot-high *Tyrannosaurus*. But it is reasonable to assume that all the members of these races of large dinosaurs perished in the Flood. Man still had a destiny before him, and God knew that he could not compete with such colossal forms."

[Ibid. P.156]

In the final part of your comment, you believe that the size of the dinosaurs would have prevented them from boarding the Ark. Most people, hold to the belief that all dinosaurs were huge. However, any *Dinosaur Encyclopedia* will help us to discover that dinosaurs came in all shapes and sizes. They range from the *Microraptor* to the 157 foot long *Breviparopus*. God placed some of the small dinosaurs on board the Ark as *representatives of the basic dinosaur kind*. The *carnivores and the extremely large dinosaurs* were left outside. **Other creation scientists, who believe that the large dinosaurs were housed in the Ark, do not believe that size was a factor. *The large dinosaurs could have sailed on the Ark while they were still juveniles or in the form of eggs.***

*WHAT ABOUT THE SO-CALLED PREHISTORIC CAVE MEN, THE CAVE DRAWINGS, ETC.?

ANSWER:

[This is the answer to the third portion of inquiries]

You refer to the prehistoric cave men as "so-called." This indicates that you have a doubt as to their existence. I do not have much time to speak of the cave men, which is a subject for another time.

However, I will say that some of these people had an authentic existence such as Neanderthal man and Cro-Magnon man. But evolutionists have been constrained to make these fossil remains (who were truly men) and others **(who were not truly men such as Zinjanthropus, Australopithecus, etc.)** fit their concept that humans evolved from ape-like creatures called **hominoids**. These alleged beings are believed to have split off into the **subpopulations of gorilla, man, chimpanzee, gibbon, and the orangutan**.

The cave men probably consisted of those bands of individuals that were scattered far from civilization and lost contact with the civilized ways of life. They, no doubt, were a fringe-society and the farther they wandered, the more barbaric and debased they became.

On the other hand, you ask, "What about the cave drawings?" There are post-flood caves in which there are drawings of Ice Age animals such as the wooly mammoth, the bison, the saber tooth cat, and others. These animals have been drawn by authentic cave men.

However, although I believe that there were certain dinosaurs, which came off the Ark, I do not know of any dinosaurs sketched on cave walls or ceilings. Caves were probably washed out shortly after the Flood. Over the course of time, the lime would turn to stone. It took awhile for the descendants of Noah and his three sons to degenerate into cave men possibly through interbreeding. This "fringe society" that branched off, for one reason or another from the main cultures, was not on the same level of intelligence or culture with other humans. It was the descendants of these cavemen who, during the Ice Age became more developed and drew pictures on the cave walls to demonstrate, among other things, their prowess in hunting. The reason that dinosaurs are not depicted on any of the cave walls, dinosaurs were not included on their hunting list. No doubt, by the time the cave walls had been hardened enough to serve as surfaces for pictures of animals, human beings had advanced to the point where this fringe society were actually drawing pictures of animals in caves. The dinosaurs could have died out and became extinct during the frigid time of the Ice Age when food was difficult to come by and dinosaurs did not have the proper survival characteristics. That is all I have to say for this evening but I do thank you for your questions and comments.

QUESTIONS SIXTEEN AND SEVENTEEN:

MR. PITTACK! WHAT IS THE BEHEMOTH IN THE BOOK OF JOB AND CHAPTER 40? I HAVE HEARD IT MENTIONED SOMEPLACE THAT THIS IS A DINOSASUR. DID JOB SEE A DINOSAUR IN HIS DAY?

ANSWER:

[This came in by the hand microphone. It is the most frequently posited question. I added the last part, "Did Job see a dinosaur in his day?" for the sake of my readers. I thought you might like to know my response]

The description of this animal is like no other animal that has been described on earth. Let us read the portion of scripture recorded in Job 40:15-24 KJV:

15 Behold now behemoth, which I made with thee; he eateth grass as an ox.

16 Lo now, his strength is in his loins, and his force is in the navel of his belly.

17 He moveth his tail like a cedar; the sinews of his stones are wrapped together.

18 His bones are as strong pieces of brass; his bones are like bars of iron.

19 He is the chief of the ways of God; he that made him can make his sword approach unto him.

20 Surely the mountains bring him forth food, where all the beasts of the fields play.

21 He lieth under the shady trees, in the covert of the reed, and fens.

22 The shady trees cover him with their shadow; the willows of the brook compass him about.

23 Behold, he drinketh up a river, and hasteth not: he trusteth that he can draw up Jordon into his mouth.

22 He taketh it with his eyes: his nose pierceth through snares.

Years ago, I was amazed when I looked up the word *Behemoth* in *the Westminster Dictionary of the Bible.* The dictionary related the fact: this is a Hebrew word meaning *"beast"* and the word was an intensive plural to denote magnitude. Thus *Behemoth* is often translated **"a beast par excellence."** But as I continued to read, expecting to gain insight from comments on this passage, I was astounded to discover *Behemoth* was thought to be none other than **the hippopotamus of the Nile River**.

Looking for further comments, I researched definitions in other dictionaries only to discover the description of the *Behemoth* was interpreted **as an elephant**. But neither the elephant nor the hippo was a suitable alternative to meet the animal portrayed in the 40th chapter of Job. The life form described by Job was much larger than any mere pachyderm. Therefore, it did not make sense to equate pachyderms with the *Behemoth* since **the tail of the Behemoth is comparative to a *cedar tree* (verse 17).**

[At the time of my meetings, I showed two pictures. The one picture was the tail of an elephant. The other picture was of a sauropod's tail. As soon as the audience concluded its laughter, I carried on with the answer. The audience immediately observed the elephant's tail (a hippo tail would look similar to that of an elephant) had no semblance to a cedar tree]

The *Behemoth, to* my way of thinking, is a sauropod dinosaur. For example, the "thunder-lizard" named *Sauroposeidon.* "Thunder-lizard" derives its name from the Greek god associated with earthquakes. I have a newspaper article which states: this dinosaur "would create a little seismic activity when it walked."

The description of Job 40:15-24 fits the description of *Sauroposeidon* or sauropods of similar genera. A sauropod was the type of dinosaur, which had a large body and an enormous neck and tail.

[I showed a picture of the *Sauroposeidon* to the audience since I believed this or something similar, is the animal which is delineated in the book of Job]

You may think the writer to have overdone his poetic license or freedom but we should remember that verse one of chapter forty reads, "Moreover the Lord answered Job and said…" This was the second, divine discourse that Jehovah spoke to Job. I grant the language is highly poetic *but what God is describing is not a mythical being but one of His own creations.* God was demonstrating His greatness as Creator by giving to Job a vision of God's work on the sixth day of creation. The representation of *Behemoth* is explicit rather than implicit. Mark Isaak (the evolutionist) likens the *Behemoth* to a bull and its virility but the portion of scripture in Job is describing a larger animal. **Only the dinosaur could be considered "the chief ways of God" and "he drinketh up a river" can only fit the dinosaur as an exaggerated expression of his thirst** – not the bull of folklore, as Isaak contends. Also, I doubt Job would have been impressed with the power of God through the creation of a bull. In verse 19, the phrase "chief of the ways of God" indicates this was **the largest land animal God had made. The tail swaying "like a cedar," is only a part of the entire portrayal of this animal. The similes of this portion of Scripture match, in every way, the known anatomy of the sauropod.**

Some creationist commentators believe Job was actually viewing *a living dinosaur.* They derive this idea from verse 15 wherein God said, "***Behold now behemoth***, which I made" but this is quoted out of context. We need to consider the entire verse: "Behold now Behemoth *which I made with thee.*" When God made this comment, he was not insinuating that Job was created at the same time Behemoth was created, *except in the inclusive sense.*

God was using "thee" to identify Job with the making of the man Adam on the sixth day of creation. This makes perfectly good sense to me while the other idea, dinosaurs – especially sauropods – **could possibly survive the Ice Age and be living in the time of Job and his environment, makes absolutely no sense at all.** The Lord was asking Job to "consider now Behemoth, which I made with thee." That is, "Job, consider for a moment the Behemoth I made along with **thee (mankind)** on the 6th day of creation." I hold to the concept that no sauropods were alive at the time of Job, due to the preceding Ice Age.

A religious writer has commented:

"There was a class of very large animals which perished at the flood. God knew that the strength of man would decrease, and that these mammoth animals could not be controlled by feeble man."

Selected Messages, Book 4

E. G. White

P.121

"Very large" was not necessarily an evil characteristic. The sauropods were not taken into the Ark only because feeble man who was weakened by sin could not control them. **I agree with the above statement of White: the large creatures such as the sauropod dinosaurs were kept off the Ark**. This fact would not be in disagreement with Genesis 6:17-20 and 7:14-16. The dinosaur kind was represented as *a land animal* on the Ark but only by the non-violent, the small, and the more docile dinosaurs. The larger dinosaurs and the rapacious killers were kept off the Ark. The dinosaur kind, therefore, would be in keeping with the above-mentioned verses and still be in harmony with the White statement.

Finally, I am convinced that Job lived under patriarchal conditions, *in or near the desert*, and after the Ice Age. Also, since I believe that **no dinosaur could have survived the Ice Age or could have lived in the desert;** God's invitation for Job to "look at the behemoth" (verse 15) was accomplished by **a supernatural appearance**. That is, a **vision** of the "par excellent beast" – the *Sauroposeidon* (or some other such sauropod).

What is inconceivable to me: the actual belief in *late and literal dinosaur sightings*. Some scholars claim that the book of Malachi (written in the 5th century B.C.) describing "dragons of the wilderness" in verse three of chapter one, are to be equated with dinosaurs. The incredible part: these alleged dinosaurs were supposed to be living in the wilderness. *The wilderness is mostly equated with the desert*.

How is it that dinosaurs – especially sauropods – found enough food in the desert environment? How many high trees would there have been to forage for this sauropod whose head was 60 feet above the ground? *A sauropod would have to eat 300 pounds of food a day if cold-blooded or a ton a day if warm-blooded.* In the time of Job, there was more than enough food to feed his livestock but enough food to feed foraging sauropods, often traveling in herds, I think not.

Surely, the dinosaur viewed by Job was not a living dinosaur but had existence only in vision. God enabled Job, for encouragement, to look back in time. Job needed to be reminded how great God was in the first week of creation and that he was still in control of Job's present and future life. Job, in vision, beheld the dinosaur and was directed to God as the Mighty Creator. Job's attention was guided to God and His greatness. And, as a student of nature, **Job knew that such a large creature could not possibly exist in a desert surrounding and, therefore, must be making a supernatural appearance.**

QUESTION EIGHTEEN:

DO THE ICA STONES SHOW THAT HUMANS AND DINOSAURS COEXISTED?

ANSWER:

[This question has nothing to do with any held meetings and is simply a point of interest for this book. In fact, I did not know about the Ica Stones until quite recently. I had to ponder this question for several days before being ready to give a response]

Andesite is enormously abundant among the intrusive rocks of the globe. It is one of the chief products of the volcanoes that form the circle of fire surrounding the Pacific Ocean. Andesite rocks got their name from the **Andes of South America**. They are many colors; **dark grey and black are common** (See *Physical Geology* by Longwell, Knopf, and Flint, third edition, p.569).

In 1966, a neighboring native gave Dr. Javier Cabrera Darquea; a home physician located in the vicinity of the village of Ica in Peru, for his birthday, a small Andesite stone. The doctor was enchanted by a hand-etched drawing of a primitive fish on the surface of the stone and because of his immense interest in the sketch; inhabitants of the region brought other stones, which they gathered from a certain riverbank. Cabrera's collection reached an astonishing 15,000 stones and became known as the ICA STONES. They "show ancient drawings of humans hunting or otherwise interacting with living dinosaurs" (Berlitz, C. 1984. *Atlantis, the Eighth Continent.* New York: Putnam, quoted by Mark Isaak in "The Counter – Creationism Handbook" p.242).

Mark Isaak attempts to demonstrate the fallacious nature of the ICA STONES by quoting M. Polidoro (2002):

"The stones are almost certainly modern created by local villagers to sell to gullible tourists. Two peasants from Callango, Basilio Uchuya and his wife, Irma Gutierrez de Aparcana, have admitted to carving the stones they sold to Cabrera, basing their designs on illustrations from comic books, school books, and magazines."

The Counter – Creationism Handbook

P.242

What Isaak fails to bring to our attention?

*The modern stone carvings have nothing to do with Cabrera's original collection found by local natives in a riverbank.

*The original ICA STONES contained nature's varnish in the grooves of the etchings indicating that the stones were very old.

*The **modern stones** did not contain varnish on the etchings. But the reproductions could not serve as evidence to detract from the fact: the **ancient ICA STONES** contained drawings of humans interacting with dinosaurs. Therefore, the modern stones do not prove the original ICA STONES to be a hoax. On the *original stones* the varnish had to be scraped away to make possible the etchings and some reports attested to *additional varnish*; indicating that the ICA STONES were **not modern pictures** of humans and dinosaurs but much older.

(The above three facts are a digest from The Billy Lids, Page 2 of 5, 6/14/2007)

Isaak brings up another point that seemingly negates the position of creationism. What is the position? – Guarantee of a young-earth should the ICA STONES prove to be a valid witness. But the authenticity of the stones could be proved only through geological dating. However, Isaak claims "the stones cannot be dated without knowing their source, and their source has never been revealed." Even creationists confess that "accidental erosion" has caused the stones to be *found in a riverbank*. **Thus, their source is unknown**. The *in situ or natural position* of the rocks, in which they were originally formed, remains a mystery. If the stones cannot be dated, the argument existing between creationists and evolutionists is pointless. On the one hand, the creationist reasoning for a young earth is **worthless** since there is absolutely no basis to prove this theory one way or the other. On the other hand, the evolutionist reasoning that the original ICA STONES centers in a modern hoax, is left **unproven** since there is a dating problem. As a creationist I remain skeptical, not to the fact of dinosaurs interacting with humans but to the truth and validity of the ICA STONES since:

1) They cannot be dated. Even though the varnish may attest to the fact the ICA STONES are old, **the varnish does not indicate how old.**

2) The late Dr. Cabrera had such fantastic notions regarding the ICA STONES. For example, the stones are a record of an advanced civilization that fled to another planet. Who were these people? Why did they leave us such crude records? With all due respect, this sounds like **a fantasy** and without any substance to support it.

3) The **supposedly *advanced civilization***, which created the stones, portrays hunting dinosaurs with *primitive weapons*.

4) Men are depicted on the Ica stones as looking through *telescopes* at the heavens (Picture in The Billy Lids, Page 4 of 5). [Pittack's Special Note: the telescopes were refractors invented in the beginning of the 17th century. If these people had such an advanced civilization, which enabled them to go from planet to planet, then **why not study the heavens through the more advanced telescopes** rather than through a simple hand-held telescope? Furthermore, are the things brought into focus with their telescopes, really objects that would normally be viewed in astronomy? The things upon which the men are focusing are *land objects* such as bodies of water, birds, trees, etc. The telescopes are simple hand-held land instruments; **not exactly the advanced and more powerful telescopes for viewing distant galaxies**. There is only one object sketched on Andesite stone that has anything to do with astronomy something that **appears to be a**

comet. But it is so **crudely inscribed** that it is only by **a stretch of the imagination** that one is able to determine the scene, etched on the Ica stone; being the art-creation of **an advanced civilization**]

The above-mentioned reasons, furnish enough evidence for me to remain unconvinced about the genuine nature of the ICA STONES.

QUESTION NINETEEN:

DO THE DINOSAUR FIGURINES FROM ACAMBARO, MEXICO DEMONSTRATE THAT MAN AND DINOSAURS WERE CONTEMPORANEOUS?

ANSWER:

[This is another question that has nothing to do with past dinosaur meetings but since some creationists have made the dinosaur figurines a major issue of the evolution-creation debates, I have no other choice but to respond to the question]

In 1944 the German hardware merchant, Waldemar Julsrud, was riding his horse on Bull (El Toro) Mountain and discovered unusual figurines. These ceramic figures were found in Acambaro, Mexico and were later known as the "Acambaro Figures" which numbered over thirty thousand. What made this archaeological discovery so unusual: many of the clay and stone figurines are perceived as dinosaurs.

[See Dr. Dennis Swift, http://en.wikipedia.org/wiki/Acambaro figures]

The species, according to some, are so perfectly depicted, scientists fail to understand how an ancient culture was able to acquire knowledge of dinosaur anatomy far superior to what has been discovered in modern days. **According to others, in some of the figures presented as dinosaurs, takes wild imagination to envisage such a resemblance.** There is, for example, a sauropod with single spikes running up and down its back. **This characteristic is not a feature of a sauropod dinosaur but more like a stegosaur.** *The stegosaurs possessed an array of spikes and thin, narrow, armor plates of bone arranged along the length of their backbone* (Stephen A. Czerkas).

Also, there is a creature that has a dinosaur's body but its head has bony "horns" which stick out sideways in the shape of a boomerang. There is only one creature that I know of that fits this description – **the *Diplocaulus*.** This animal was an amphibian, which had a body much like a newt or salamander. Dozens of these fossils have been collected and the specimens that are fully-grown have skulls, which are 9 inches wide. **[It was a swimming creature; NOT A DINOSAUR]** The horns were outgrowths of the bones that make up the cheek area of the skull and they would keep larger animals from swallowing *Diplocaulus.*

[See Dr. Michael Benton's book *Dinosaur and Other Prehistoric Animal Fact Finder*, p.92]

Apparently the artists of the figurines did not consider size since the animals were not fashioned proportionately. I must admit, as a creationist, I find it difficult to accept these fashioned images as true products of what was actually seen by the artists and not the **creation of their imagination**. In other words, some of the figures that are represented as dinosaurs **fall short in their resemblance. On the other hand, it would be expected to have some figurines, out of a collection of thirty thousand variations, look like dinosaurs.** This is a personal observation of John Blanton in *The Acambaro Dinosaurs,* "Metareligion", and Oct.1999 – Blanton writes, "It's possible we are seeing some selective sampling. Given the amount of variation apparent in the collection they're bound to be a dinosaur in there somewhere." I must agree with the logic of his remark.

Nevertheless, some creationists make the following claims since thermo luminescence tests indicate the figures were made 6,500 years ago and long before modern science discovered dinosaurs:

1) The dinosaur figurines demonstrate that ancient people were familiar with dinosaurs.

2) Some of the ceramic figurines not only resemble dinosaurs but the likeness is beyond all doubt. In fact, the figures are said to resemble dinosaurs drawn by Robert Bakker in his book, *Dinosaur Heresies* (see Dennis Swift cited above).

[Bakker is an artist-scientist who specializes in dinosaurology and is an evolutionist]

3) The figures are impeccable evidence for the coexistence of dinosaurs and humans.

4) The Acambaro Figures prove to be, in some cases, up to 6,500 years old by thermo luminescent radiocarbon dating. Cultures that created these animal figurines must have had first hand experience by living in the same environmental setting, as did the dinosaurs. The artist or artists must have seen dinosaurs in the flesh.

5) If the Acambaro Figures were genuine, then this would throw the entire Geological Time Scale off course and prove man and dinosaurs were not separated by long periods of time. This, in turn, would attest to a young earth and would unveil the fallacious doctrine of evolutionary deep time.

After the finds made by Julsrud, it was difficult to find scholars and scientists interested in making an assessment of the figurines. Once they heard about the dinosaur-man connection, their prejudices were immediately triggered and they refused to take the discovery of the figurines serious enough to warrant investigation. After all, most people know that man did not appear on the earth until over sixty million years after the demise of the dinosaur kingdoms. Evolutionists are so unerring in their science-philosophy, anything contradicting their steadfast belief in evolution is promptly assumed to be unworthy of their consideration. Such is the folly of a self-serving attitude that turns its back on the quest of science, which evolves the act of gathering evidence and making inquiries into the nature of things to either support or contradict an original theory or proposition.

Finally, there was so much publicity surrounding the figurines; Charles C. Di Peso, an archaeologist of the American Foundation, agreed to examine the thousands of clay and stone figurines. Mark Isaak in his book, *The Counter – Creationism Handbook*, claims that this examination began in 1953. Isaak lists the main observations reported by Di Peso on page 243 of his book. Of course, they are very much one-sided and in favor of evolution. *Brackets containing counter arguments will follow the main observations:*

1) The surfaces of the figurines were new and not marred by patina. No dirt was packed in any of the crevices. The eyes and mouth of each figurine were sharp, clear, and new.

[However, Dr. J. Antonio Villia Hennejon personally excavated ceramic artifacts from 1950 to 1955. He claimed that in 1951, he and Julsrud cleaned up the artifacts that were encrusted with dirt and patina. Tinejero and other helpers completed the job. Eyewitnesses were present at the time of the excavation of these figurines and confirmation was given by them to **verify the artifacts did have dirt and patina. Patina is a colored film or thin layer produced on the surface of rock by weathering]**

2) The 32,000 items in pristine condition is unheard of for genuine archaeological relics. Di Peso reports that the excavators were "neither careful nor experienced" yet there appeared no shovel, pick, or mattocks marks on the 32,000 specimens. Some figurines were broken to suggest age but the breaks were unworn and no parts were missing.

[However, Don Patton (a young-earth creationist) has provided what he claims to be accurate **radiocarbon dates ranging from 6,500 years to 1,500 years. Other tests have been done on the figurines, which have them dated from approximately 2,500 B.C.]**

3) The story of the figurines discovery gives a motive for fraud. Waldemar Julsrud paid workers a peso apiece for intact figurines.

[However, the ceramic collection has won the admiration of professional artists. **No peasants and modern day farmers could possibly make thousands and thousands of non–duplicated sculptures.** It is almost impossible to explain the figures were planted as a hoax by farmers and disguised as ancient artifacts]

Mark Isaak has placed a great deal of confidence in Di Peso's report of 1953, which is counter-creationism. But there are others who see this report as biased, outrageous, deceptive, and based on mere conjecture. For example, John H. Tierney points out that **Di Peso could not possibly have minutely examined 32,000 pieces in the stated time of 5 hours.** It would have taken weeks for a proper evaluation. According to Tierney, Di Peso would have had to inspect 133 pieces per minute steadily for four hours. In the summer of 1955, Charles Hapgood excavated sites on undisturbed ground and even received permission to dig under the floor of a house built in 1930, long before artifacts were found on Bull Hill. He unearthed dozens of these "Julsrud type figurines." This finds cleared Julsrud of manufacturing his own discoveries and negated Di Peso's report of 1953.

The time has come to offer, for whatever it is worth, my evaluation of the "Acambaro Figures." Before I do so, it is necessary to weigh in on both sides of the "scale of decision" with the *pro* and *con* facts. **Firstly, the positive aspects for the side of creationism will be dealt with in the following manner:**

PRO:

Di Peso has been called an intelligent and crafty professional. But are we going to consider his intelligent level so high that he could examine 32,000 figures of art in the space of a few short hours and determine they were not authentic but rather the product of local, modern day farmers. Other professionals contradicted his 1953 report (Charles Hapgood, Don Patton, Dennis Swift, John H. Tierney, Carlos Perea, Juan Terrazaz Carranza, etc.). **There are known incidents that discredit the Di Peso observations:**

1) The report that the artifacts were in the ground for a short period of time is not valid. Tree roots, at a depth of five or six feet, entwined the objects and proved them to be very old and therefore **contradicted the report.** [See *The Dinosaurs of Acambaro*, initial report by Dr Dennis Swift Ph.D., ^http://www.bible.ca/tracks/tracks-acambaro.htm]

2) On July 23, 1952, Juan Carranza (the Municipal President of Acambaro) issued an official statement; no ceramic activity had taken place in the last four years. **The statement counteracted Di Peso's allegation.**

3) The excavated sites in 1955 by Charles Hapgood and his discoveries of "Julsrud type figures" under a house built in 1930, exonerated Julsrud of manufacturing his own discoveries, **a direct negation of Di Peso's report of 1953**.

The thermo luminescent tests by the University of Pennsylvania of 18 samples, which gave 2,500 B.C. on the average before the technicians, discovered that ceramic models of dinosaurs were being tested and retracted the dating. **Dennis Swift claims the labs made the retraction** (See ^http://www.bible.ca/tracks/tracks-acambaro.htm).

[The eventual denial and retraction of the testing results speaks to me of the strong prejudicial feelings held by some evolutionists. **According to the above incident, dating tests are reliable only when they nicely fit into the theory of evolution.** The minute that testing fits the theory of creation, such testing must be denied and retracted]

The dinosaur figurines do not appear to be dragging their tails. This characteristic is difficult to explain from the evolutionary perspective. If the figurines are fraudulent, then how did the modern natives of the 1940s know about this special characteristic? And if the objects were made by the preclassical Chupicuaro Culture: 800 B.C.E. to 200 C.E. (Isaak), or even further back in time (The radiocarbon and thermo luminescent dating gives the artifacts much older dates), **then the artist or artists must have had firsthand observations of dinosaurs.** [We had to wait for over a hundred years after the discovery of dinosaurs for dinosaur anatomists to come up with the idea that dinosaurs did not drag their tails. They concluded that the giant tail would offset the weight of the head and trunk as the dinosaur walked. The tail was raised off the ground for a counterbalance. In other words, the tail functioned as a counterpoise to lessen the strain on the trunk]

CON:

I will now deal with the contrary elements that **I find to be rather essential arguments against the creationistic theory** regarding the "Acambaro Figures":

1) Waldemar Julsrud was supposedly aware of the various Indian civilizations. **He claimed that the figurines he held in his hand were different than any other known Indian cultures including the Tarascan.** Julsrud later claimed Di Peso was convinced of the genuineness of the collection of figurines and wanted to **purchase *pieces of Tarascan origin*. How could the figurines be different from other Indian cultures (including the Tarascan) and yet have pieces of Tarascan origin? I see this as a blatant contradiction.** Were the two cultures mixed in the excavations?

Creationists made the claim: the dinosaur figurines are from the pre-classical Chupicuaro Culture, **800 B.C. to 200 A.D.** Mark Isaak, from the evolutionist position, claims that the "figurines are not from the Chupicuaro. **They came from within a single-component**

Tarascan ruin. The Tarascan are post-classical and historical, emerging between **900 and 1522 C.E."**

[Special Note: **Neither culture extends far enough back in time to have the artists of the figurines see dinosaurs in the flesh.** Some creationists believe dinosaurs to have existed up to the middle ages but this position can be questioned since most dinosaurs met their death during the Great Flood and many others, which were post-flood, finally became extinct during the Ice Age]

2) Some creationists claim that dinosaur figurines, numbering several hundred, were *scientifically identified* as representing many *species of dinosaurs*. This may be true of some figures CONSIDERED TO BE DINOSAURS **but not true of all figures since the identification list contains species of OTHER ANIMALS IDENTIFIED AS DINOSAURS BUT ARE NOT DINOSAURS.** The examples of species: I have taken the liberty of making corrections with CAPITAL LETTERS:

Ichthyornis is A BIRD – not a dinosaur.

Dimetrodon is A SAIL-BACKED. MAMMAL-LIKE REPTILE – not a dinosaur.

Pteranodon and *Rhamphorhyncus* ARE FLYING REPTILES – not dinosaurs.

Plesiosaur was A SEA REPTILE – not a dinosaur.

Leviathan was A MYTHOLOGICAL SEA SERPENT – not a dinosaur. [The reader can refer to QUESTION THIRTY-TWO: IS LEVIATHAN IN THE BOOK OF JOB, A DINOSAUR?]

3) If the artists of the dinosaur figurines were actually acquainted with these creatures and saw them in their natural setting, then why have no dinosaur fossils been found in the Acambaro region throughout all Mexico? Why did no other Mexican cultures record any dinosaurs? **These two questions seem to invalidate the creationist argument: originators of the artifacts must have been eyewitnesses, who discovered dinosaurs in their natural setting.** There are maps of the localities of dinosaur discoveries worldwide. For example, Pp.198-199 in *The Illustrated Encyclopedia of Dinosaurs* (an original and compelling insight into life in the dinosaur kingdom), written by Dr David Norman, provides such information. The only dinosaur, which has known to be associated with Mexico, is the *Diplodocus* cast located in the Natural History Museum of Mexico City. Please do not confuse *Diplodocus* (the dinosaur) with *Diplocaulus* (the amphibian, which had a body much like a newt or salamander)!

[Special Note: The *Diplodocus* was one of the many dinosaur species identified in the Acambaro figurines. The reason this dinosaur was called "double Beam," it describes an unusual feature of the backbone. There were small bones below the backbone, which had a piece running forward and backward and thus, a "double beam." In other words, the chevron bones, which hang beneath the tail vertebrae, gave the reinforcement and probably enabled this creature to raise its tail from off the ground. This unique feature has also been noted in *Apatosaurus* and *Cetiosauriscus*]

Being fully aware that in this section I should be dealing with things that are contrary to creationistic viewpoints, I cannot help but mention this one fact. Is it not a strange coincidence: the dinosaur figurines are not dragging their tail? This strange concurrence seems to have been known by the originators of the ceramic Acambaro Figures. This anomaly is difficult to explain. **Nevertheless, no dinosaur fossils have been found in Mexico and this remains a substantial argument against the creationists' position.**

4) I have already mentioned *Diplocaulus,* the amphibian with the boomerang-like skull and the sauropod with single spikes running up and down its back. **These are not like any known dinosaurs and the animals appear to be product of the imagination and not fashioned after the actual visualization of dinosaurs allegedly seen by the artists.**

5) Accounts seem to indicate that Waldemar Julsrud did not do any of the uncovering of the figurines. If this is indeed true and the hired Mexican farmer and helpers brought to Julsrud the 32,000 figures, **then it is a more certain case he opened himself to fraud. Thus, the genuineness of the ceramic artifacts would be more in doubt.** Di Peso actually witnessed parts of the excavation and attests there was previous tampering with the site. He claims that he "examined the material *in situ.* The black fill dirt of the prehistoric room had very recently buried the cache. This fill ran to a depth of approximately 1.30 m. **Within the stratum there were authentic Tarascan shards, obsidian blades, tripod metates, manos, etc., but these objects held no concern for the excavators.** In burying the cache of figurines, the natives had unwittingly cut some 15 cms below the black fill into the sterile red earth floor of the prehistoric room. In back-filling the tunnel they mixed this red sterile earth with black earth; the tracing of their original excavation was, as a result, a simple task."

[Quote is taken from Mark Isaak's book "The Counter-Creationism Handbook" and page 243]

[The Julsrud type figurine discovered by Charles Hapgood under the floor of a house built in 1930 does not necessarily offset the previous tampering of the excavation at Bull Mountain in 1944]

In order to believe the details of the discovery of the Acambaro Figures, **we are left at the mercy of men who were witnesses and gave their reports.** Some of these men were creationists and others were evolutionists. Who are we going to believe? To the evolutionist, every creationist is a liar and his reports are based on faulty information and false-science. To the creationist, every evolutionist is an atheist and their reports are not only filled with dishonesty and deception but are never to be trusted, not even one time. Has science come down to this: wherein we poor laymen are left to depend on the reports of men and left to make our decisions based upon whatever personal philosophy we happen to hold dear? One man says, "I am a creationist so whatever reports are made up by creationism scientists, I will believe them." Another man may say, "I am an evolutionist so whatever reports are made up by evolutionism scientists, I will believe them." **No small wonder, when it comes to the Acambaro Figures, I am left in a dilemma. I appeal to my readers the necessity of making an honest attempt to find out all the available information before making a particular decision.**

I have considered some of the positive and negative elements in the find of the ceramic dinosaurs. There are simply not enough green lights to help me make a decision favoring the authenticity of the earthenware dinosaurs. **However, creationists do not need to find examples of dinosaurs and man existing contemporaneously. Rather, they need to**

come up with explanations why human fossils are not discovered in more abundance.

I feel that the entire case of the Acambaro Figures is centered on dating tests. I would love to have in my possession, the original thermo luminescent testing results by unbiased technologists. If such dating would carry me back to the time of the Ice Age, then I would no longer have doubts that the artists of the Acambaro Figures actually beheld dinosaurs in the flesh. Otherwise, I will continue to keep my decision in abeyance.

SPECIAL NOTE:

In light of what I have stated about human fossils not being found in abundance and confirming the fact they existed contemporaneously with dinosaurs, I would like my readers to consider the following verses:

"But they deliberately forgot that *long* ago by God's word the heavens existed and the earth was formed out of water and by water. By these waters also the **world of that time was *deluged and destroyed.*** By the same word the present heavens and earth are reserved for fire, being kept for the Day of Judgment and *destruction of ungodly men.*"

2 Peter 3:5-7

NIV

God was not much concerned with preserving man along with the dinosaur in the fossil record as he was in carrying out his judgments in the *destruction of ungodly men.* The Biblical record does not say that man was *preserved* in the fossil record. Rather it says that men were *destroyed.* That is: men were destroyed utterly, brought to nought and were made void, deprived of life and utterly perished.

"Now the earth was corrupt in God's sight and was full of violence. God saw how corrupt the earth had become, for all the people on earth had corrupted their ways. So God said to Noah, I am going to put an *end to all people*, for the earth is filled with violence because of them. I am surely going to *destroy both them and the earth*."

Genesis 6:11-13

NIV

The Bible teaches that the Flood was **a world-destroying and men-destroying event**. Man was destroyed **with** the earth and not **from** the earth. In the Bible, the total destruction of the human race by the Flood is made evident. The purpose of the Flood was *to **wipe out and destroy*** a sinful and degenerate humanity; not *to preserve it.*

The following is a brief excerpt from the chapter entitled "After the Flood" from the book, *Patriarchs and Prophets* by Ellen G. White. Chapters seven and eight of this same book (THE FLOOD-7; AFTER THE FLOOD-8) are the very best accounts of the events which occurred at the time of the Flood and the effects which followed it. I have never read these chapters without having the feeling that I was actually present at the time the Flood took place:

"The entire surface of the earth was changed at the flood. A third dreadful curse rested upon it in consequence of sin. As the water began to subside a vast turbid sea surrounded the hills and mountains. Everywhere were strewn the dead bodies of man and beasts. The

Lord would not permit these to remain to decompose and pollute the air; therefore he made of the earth a vast burial-ground. A violent wind which was caused to blow for the purpose of drying up the waters moved them with great force, in some instances even carrying away the tops of the mountains and heaping up trees, rocks, and earth above the bodies of the dead."

Ellen G. White

Patriarchs and Prophets

Pp.107-108

Justice and love demanded God's judgments should put a check on sin. Thus, men were destroyed in the black depths of the Flood. In Genesis 6:17, God said, "And behold, even I, do bring a flood of waters upon the earth, to destroy all flesh, wherein is the breath of life ..." The words, "even I," demonstrates that the judgments of God *seem contrary* to His nature of love. However, love was evidenced in His preservation of the righteous Noah and his family [his ancestors, as well] who, for a season, would not have to suffer under the cruel influence and cold-blooded crimes of the wicked.

GENERAL QUESTIONS

QUESTION TWENTY:

WHAT EXACTLY IS A DINOSAUR? I WOULD LIKE TO KNOW THE BACKGROUND OF ITS NAME.

ANSWER:

[This is a common question answered during the course of my lectures]

I take the question to mean: what are the outstanding characteristics, which make a dinosaur different from animals of the past or present? Firstly, I will respond to the background of the name. Where did the name originate? The word "dinosaur" is not mentioned in the Bible. The Bible was written over a period of 1600 years by forty different men, from 1500 years before Christ to the end of the first century A.D.

The Fourth Gospel was written at or about the end of the first century and the word *Dinosauria* was coined over 1700 years later. Richard Owen reached the conclusion that three of the creatures, *Megalosaurus, Iguanodon*, and *Hylaeosaurus* were prehistoric reptiles belonging to previously unrecognized group of animals he called *Dinosauria*. This is a compound Greek word: *deinos* meaning "terrible' and *sauros* meaning "lizard."

Owen first announced this name at the British Association for the Advancement of Science annual meeting in Plymouth, England, in 1841 (*The Book Of Dinosaurs, The Natural History Of Museum Guide,* Tim Gardom with Angela Milner, p.94).

However, some writers on creationism will tell you that every time the word "dragon" appears in the Bible, it stands for "dinosaur." [See my response to QUESTION THIRTY: dragons are not dinosaurs in the biblical sense]

In fact, some creationists have identified dinosaurs with swamp creatures, Pterosaurs, sea monsters, serpents, and the *Leviathan* of Job 41. However, modern studies in dinosaurology have established dinosaurs to be land animals. Most creationists believe dinosaurs were called into existence on the sixth day of creation (Genesis 1:24-25). The only other valid biblical identification is found in the fortieth chapter of the book of Job. *Behemoth* was definitely a *sauropod dinosaur*, which appeared to Job in vision.

[See my response to QUESTIONS SIXTEEN AND SEVENTEEN]

Secondly, what is a dinosaur? Before going into that, we need to understand *the following creatures are not dinosaurs*:

A *Leviathan* (Job 41; Psalms 104:26; Isaiah 27:1; Job 3:8; Psalms 74:14) IS NOT A DINOSAUR:

*It is associated with Ugaritic Texts and is described as a *twisting serpent*, often appearing in folklore as a mythical creature.

*According to Job 41, it cannot be captured, tamed, killed, or eaten by man. Therefore, it is no ordinary animal and must be considered as mythical.

*It is clearly described as a SEA REPTILE and thus, NOT AS A DINOSAUR. *Ichthyosaurs*, *Plesiosaurs*, and *Mosasurs* were NOT DINOSAURS – they were SEA-REPTILES.

A pterodactyl such as *Pterodactylus* is NOT A DINOSAUR:

*It is a flying archosaur and although dinosaurs were members of the archosaurs they are distinct from all other archosaurs for one main reason – they were able to walk and run with extreme efficiency. But dinosaurs could not fly. A pterodactyl COULD FLY and is, therefore, NOT A DINOSAUR.

A plesiosaur is NOT A DINOSAUR:

*It has already been mentioned as a sea-reptile. Dinosaurs were land-dwelling animals and not marine creatures.

So, what is a dinosaur? I will repeat what Don Lessem has said on page 11 of *Time for Learning Dinosaurs*. His is the best short but precise run-down I have ever come across. Dinosaurs did not share the following features with other animals, mentioned in QUESTION TWELVE:

*They had three vertebrae in the sacrum area.

*A thighbone held straight beneath the body.

*A twisted shinbone.

*A birdlike foot and …

*A very small forth finger of the hand.

Also dinosaurs were divided into two groups by their hip structure. Don Lessem adds what does not appear in QUESTION TWELVE:

"Ornithischian plant eaters of bird-hipped dinosaurs had two of their three hip bones pointing forward and linked closely together. Saurischians or Lizard-hipped dinosaurs included giant plant eaters and all meat eaters. Their hips had a pubic bone pointing downward."

[Ibid. P.11]

Added Note: The *Leviathan* of Job 41 cannot be identified with a dinosaur since the *Leviathan* is a sea monster and the dinosaur is a land animal. The *Behemoth of Job 40 is strictly a land creature that goes down to the water to drink.* A sea creature does not "lieth under the shady trees" (verse 21). *Behemoth* is definitely a sauropod. Except for the poetic liberty the writer of Job uses, the description fits perfectly any sauropod species.

QUESTION TWENTY- ONE:

DO DINOSAUR CLASSIFICATION SYSTEMS AND THE NEW STUDY OF CLADISTICS PROVE THE EVOLUTION OF DINOSASURS?

ANSWER:

[This question is a personalized question made for this book]

Cladistic Analysis is just another attempt to solve the problem of the lack of fossil transitions. George Gaylord Simpson has described disillusioned naturalists who cannot account for 'mega-evolution' since continuous, transitional sequences are virtually absent in the fossil record.

The *older* system of classification categorized plants and animals by their overall similar characteristics. But the *new* method of classification gives each characteristic an assigned code and then is added to a computer database. Cladistics is not a new concept except in the use of computers. Keith Thompson claims that this method sends researchers on *a fool's errand* so far as finding evolutionary ancestors.

Cladistics makes more prominent the hierarchies of nested sets of groups of animals and **fails to prove that life's forms originate from a common ancestor.** All that cladistics does is map character patterns of dinosaurs and not their true relationships. **With no evolutionary proof for common ancestors, it is virtually impossible to have cladistics show dinosaur evolution** (See chapter five of Pittack's book, *The Archaeopteryx Controversy* and entitled "The Tale of Two Quests – Biochemistry and Cladistic Analysis" for a more comprehensive study of cladistics).

"In the study of cladistics: NO SPECIES CAN BE CONSIDERED ANCESTRAL TO ANY OTHER. Why? – NATURE'S ORDER IS NOT SEQUENTIAL." [Quote from Pittack's book, *The Archaeopteryx Controversy*]

QUESTION TWENTY-TWO:

I BELIEVE THAT DINOSAUR PAINTINGS AND MODELS OF DINOSAUR ARE FIGMENTS OF THE IMAGINATION AND NOTHING MORE. WE GET SO MANY CONCEPTS OF DINOSAURS FROM BONES ALONE. DID DINOSAURS TRULY EXIST?

ANSWER:

[The answer given so long ago was short compared with the following remarks. However, I am at liberty to give further insight through the lengthening of my commentary. With the few examples of dinosaur finds that will be referred to, I will set out to establish these creatures to be more than the figment of our imagination. Rather, we shall see that DINOSAURS *ARE FOR REAL*. In my conversations with friends and acquaintances, I was surprised to find there were some who did not believe in the reality of dinosaurs]

I will begin with an apropos quote from Coffin (a creationist):

"THERE WAS A TIME, when some people did not believe that dinosaurs ever really existed. But those who have collected dinosaur remains in the Midwest plains of Canada and the United States, or in the Colorado Plateau region, have no lingering doubt concerning their reality. Thousands of specimens have been found and excavated. Occasional skeletons are nearly complete, and some are in an undisturbed lifelike position. They need only to be removed from the ground and mounted in a museum.

Teeth, armor plates, and, rarely, skin are found, and these give us some concept of external appearance and type of diet. It is quite possible that some of the more detailed features of the flesh and body outline may be wrongly reconstructed, but the general shape and form are correct."

Creation – Accident or Design

Harold G. Coffin

P.184

Let us travel to **Mongolia** and discover the reality of that amazing find called "A Fight to the Finish.**" Scientists in Mongolia discovered the remains of *Velociraptor* and *Protoceratops* locked together in death.** The fossils were discovered in 1971 and constitute a most remarkable find. The dinosaurs died while engaged in combat. The beak of *Protoceratops* appears to have stuck into the chest of *Velociraptor*. During the fight, the *Velociraptor* claws dug into its enemy's head. The parrot like beak of the

Protoceratops had a sharp point that could penetrate thick skin and inflict mortal wounds. *Velociraptor* was a bigger animal and had as its main characteristic, long, sharp claws. Nevertheless, it suffered irreparable damage and bled to death, as did its enemy. *Protoceratops* skull had a bony shield spread in a curve over the back of its neck. Apparently, this means of defense was not enough to spare it in its final battle. The reality of these two dinosaurs has been demonstrated through the discovery of the bonesets of these creatures. *The intact skeletons of Protoceratops and Velociraptor* further substantiates the belief that dinosaurs were valid beings and should engender, in our mind, a more intellectual approach to their existence and an awareness of their reality.

We will now visit **New Mexico** and find out about its state fossil, *Coelophysis.* Sunset magazine of June 1987, has an excellent article entitled "Dinosaur Country" which contains a photograph of a young women working on a dinosaur specimen at Ghost Ranch, New Mexico. In the background, **a *complete skeleton of Coelophysis*** is mounted on a plaque, which is inset to accommodate the ***intact bone structure*** of this bird like creature. Ghost Ranch, located in Albuquerque, New Mexico is known for Triassic dinosaurs *preserved* in brilliantly oxidized Chinle. One area contains *hundreds of Coelophysis dinosaurs*, which probably met their death in the Great Flood. A trail at Ghost Ranch leads to this *Coelophysis quarry*. With so many discoveries of this *distinctive species of dinosaur*, it is no marvel *Coelophysis* was raised to the status of New Mexico state fossil and has *established the reality of its* existence.

Coelophysis means "hollow form" which alerts the interested to the dinosaur's hollow bones. The thin form coupled with a weight, which was not equal to that of a human adult, enabled *Coelophysis* to turn sharply and run fast to catch quickly moving prey. Edward Cope first discovered this dinosaur in 1881. Since that time, *small skeletons have been found within larger ones*, leading scientists to conclude that mothers were carrying their young or *Coelophysis* was a cannibal.

While it is a fact that many bones of this dinosaur have come out of the quarries intermingled, **it is also a fact that many skeletons of *Coelophysis* are intact when discovered. Such evidence cannot be refuted nor should it be possible to ignore such clear certainties of its fossilized survival. *Coelophysis was a real dinosaur*,** which inhabited the forests, ponds, and streams of New Mexico and the Connecticut Valley. To reject the reality of this small, meat-eating dinosaur is to deny rationality of the brain's power to produce images and the trustworthiness of sense perception.

The gruesome feeding habits of this predator have a factual basis. Most dinosaurologists believe that all dinosaurs were egg-layers rather than livebearers. This being true, it is hardly likely that the large and well-formed skeletons found in the rib cages of the adults could have come from within eggs. If dinosaurs were not livebearers, then neither could it be true that the young skeletons were unborn infants. The assumption that they represent the remains of cannibalism rather than egg embryos seems to be the only alternative explanation. *Coelophysians* were not imaginary creatures but they were certainly unusual since they devoured their own kind.

At Ghost Ranch, multitudes of beautiful skeletons are available and *Coelophysians* are among the best known of all predatory dinosaurs. When the skeletons were first discovered in 1947, they were all lying across one another. Their posture was, no doubt, the result of a catastrophic phenomenon. The *Coelophysians* number over five hundred and include all ages from the very young to fully-grown. [For detailed comments concerning this quarry and the Great Flood, the reader is directed to Pittack's book entitled *The Archaeopteryx Controversy*, chapter twelve and under the section on DINOSAUR QUARRIES]

For further evidence that dinosaurs are for real, let us visit **Rabbit Valley Quarry**. Colorado and Utah are states forming the "Great Dinosaur Triangle." The gray rock forming the landscape is the Mother Lode to paleontologists and is considered to be a *dinosaur goldmine.* **Should anyone entertain doubts concerning the existence of dinosaurs, then Rabbit Valley Quarry is the perfect place to visit. It is one of the few places you can see fossils not yet excavated from the rock.**

Camarasaurus was one of the smallest sauropods. But it was four times as long as the biggest elephant now alive and measured about forty feet from the nose to the tip of the tail. At Rabbit Valley Quarry, *you can actually, with your own eyes, see the limb bones and vertebrae of Camarasaurus still embedded in rock.*

Bones of an *Iguanodon* may also be viewed as they are firmly set in the strata for all to behold. The fitting together of these Colorado bones into the final product, classified as *Camarasaurus* and *Iguanodon*, can leave no doubt as to the accuracy of such reconstructions since *the reality of the bones themselves can hardly be questioned.* If you have but a superficial knowledge of skeletal anatomy, then you will discern the Rabbit Valley Quarry bones, in this case, belong to large animals of the past. Also, keep in mind these bones have been compared to specimens of *Camarasaurus* and *Iguanodon* found in other regions. Such comparisons make it possible for paleontologists to identify the incomplete dinosaur remains of the Rabbit Valley Quarry. We will now identify the last example for the reality of dinosaurs.

All of us are familiar with the name *Tyrannosaurus*. According to dinosaur classification, it is the genus category for this particular animal and means "Tyrant Lizard." *Tyrannosaurus* is the only dinosaur usually described with the attached species name. **In that the species category of *Tyrannosaurus* is "rex," the title lengthens to the impressive "King of Tyrant Lizards."**

In the year 1902, Dr. Barnum Brown of the American Museum of Natural History in New York had a dream come true. For years he had hoped to discover the skeleton of *Tyrannosaurus*. Bones of this mighty animal had been found in the beds of western North America as well as in Europe and Mongolia. Dr. Brown went to the **badlands of South Dakota** and after only a few days, found bones in blue sandstone. The sandstone was hard and could be broken up only through the careful placement of dynamite. Brown and his assistants made a pit twenty-five feet deep to remove the bones. The men were extremely careful in their methods and it took two summers to take out the big skeleton of *Tyrannosaurus rex*. Dr. Brown took no chances in attempting the removal of bones from the stone. Rather, he hauled the blocks of stone to the railroad and had them shipped to the New York museum. Scientists carved away the stone, reconstructed the bones, and mounted *Tyrannosaurus rex* in the great exhibit hall of the Museum of Natural History in New York. Dr. Brown's dream had, at last, materialized and "King of the Lizards" is on display for all eyes to behold and minds to marvel (See *Dinosaurs* by Ruth Wheeler and Harold G. Coffin, Pp, 55-57).

Wheeler and Coffin wrote in their account, *Dinosaurs,* of the discovery of *Tyrannosaurus rex* by Dr. Barnum Brown:

"As he dug around the bones, he found that they *lay in the shape of the animal.* The bones were not in a heap as many dinosaur bones are."

P.67 [Italics, mine]

If this account, written by two creationists, is reliable; it must be concluded Tyrannosaurus was found intact and that the great monster is no figment of some scientist's imagination. *Dinosaurs are for real* and *Tyrannosaurus rex is one more fossil to step into the witness box and, through his intact remains, testify to its reality and past existence.*

Many more examples could be given of dinosaurs found *in situ.* That is, just as they are; the bones fully articulated and not separated. From the tell-tale signs – those characteristics that are found only in dinosaur anatomy – the fossilized bones *are vivid testimonials to the reality of dinosaurs that at one time walked the earth as real life forms.*

QUESTION TWENTY-THREE:

HOW WAS IT POSSIBLE THAT SOME DINOSAURS FLEW? THEY WERE NOT SUPPOSED TO HAVE FEATHERS.

ANSWER:

[Another question by way of the hand-microphone]

I can assure you: no dinosaurs were capable of flight. And no, they did not have feathers. Some evolutionists believe that modern birds are dinosaurs. They contend the ancient and extinct bird, *Archaeopteryx*, was the missing link between lizards and birds. They even claim dinosaurs had feathers. I wrote an entire book entitled *The Archaeopteryx Controversy* and in it, the above evolutionary claims have been refuted.

People make the common mistake of linking flying reptiles with dinosaurs. Most books on evolution, flying reptiles are mentioned in the same context as dinosaurs but they do not have the same taxonomic features. Dinosaurs are not to be confused with pterosaurs. Although both animals are classified as reptiles, pterosaurs were flying archosaurs and not to be equated with the non-flying land animals – dinosaurs. Also, a DINOSAUR WAS NOT a *Dimorphodon*, a *Rhamphorhyncus phyllurus*, a *Pteranodon*, or a *Quetzalcoatlus*. These flying reptiles are not to be confused with non-flying dinosaurs.

QUESTION TWENTY-FOUR:

WAS IT TRUE THAT DINOSAURS HAD NO FEATHERS OR COVERINGS ON THEIR SKIN AND WHY?

ANSWER:

[A common question asked throughout meetings, except for the last part – Why?]

Skin impressions are hard to come by but they have been found in Red Deer River in Alberta, Canada. Complete duckbill skeletons have been uncovered which included patches of skin impressions in the sandstone. The stone recorded the skin's texture only. The skin, of course, had long been rotted. There are other specimens but no appearance of feathers or even of scales. So rare are skin impressions, it can hardly be deduced that dinosaurs had no feathers. But to believe they did sport feathers is highly speculative and is purported only by those evolutionists who believe in the *birdiness* of dinosaurs.

The pictures we see of dinosaurs are the conceptions of artists. Their paintings and drawings are called restorations. An artist can paint dinosaurs according to his or her imagination. Some artists love to paint feathers on their dinosaur restorations. But the process is not true – it is merely the product of the way artists picture things in their mind's-eye. Also, certain artists are commissioned by paleontologists to illustrate that dinosaurs had feathers.

[For my readers: On the front cover of the *National Geographic*, July 1998 is a picture of a feathered dinosaur. In fact, the subtitle is "Dinosaurs Take Wing." The article was based on the discovery of a creature called *Sinosauropteryx prima*. It was thought by investigators to have had feathers but all this idea was disproved a year later. In fact, all the so-called feathered dinosaurs found in northeastern China were proved to be false. Only one specimen demonstrated feathers and this specimen was not a feathered dinosaur but rather a flightless bird – the *Caudipteryx*. This specimen fell under the category of flightless birds rather than under cursorial dinosaurs. *Caudipteryx*, in comparison to small dinosaurs, had a relatively shorter tail, a center of gravity located in a more forward (headward) position, and relatively longer legs. It was a bird, not a dinosaur. The readers are referred to my book, *The Archaeopteryx Controversy*, and chapter nine, "The China Syndrome" – (Do Feathered Dinosaurs Truly Exist?). This will give you a complete run-down of how feathered dinosaurs were defrocked]

In answer to the question: why were dinosaurs made in this way? I would suppose the only answer that could possibly be given, without my having to proclaim omniscience –

dinosaurs were created that way by God and so far as anybody knows, only birds have wings with feathers.

QUESTION TWENTY-FIVE:

AS A CREATIONIST, I CANNOT BRING MYSELF TO BELIEVE THAT GOD WOULD CREATE VICIOUS MEAT-EATING DINOSAURS. I DON'T THINK THERE IS ANY EVIDENCE THERE WERE CARNIVOROUS DINOSAURS. IS IT CORRECT TO ASSUME THE FOSSIL RECORD PROVES THAT DINOSAURS WERE VEGETARIANS?

ANSWER:

[Out of all the questions submitted by the audience, this one was the most surprising. The first statement did not shock me. This is a perfectly, logical assumption for anyone who believes in a loving Creator. What amazed me, the second statement and then the question that follows it. With all the predatory creatures alive today on planet earth; it was difficult for me to visualize the dinosaur kingdoms and especially, after sin and the fall of man, as consisting only of herbivorous dinosaurs with no natural enemies. But I sensed the urgency of the question and the sincerity, which backed it]

I understand where you are coming from and I can relate to your feelings. It is difficult for us to imagine a God of love ruling over the time of dinosaur cruelty, to reconcile death mechanics with the hand of life extended over God's created works, to look back on the so-called Mesozoic Era and imagine the numerous dead carcasses scattered throughout the various landscapes. The evolutionists, unlike us, I perceive as having a stoic and cold response to this time of horror in the natural world. To them, the world of tooth-and-claw is simply the expected result of evolution, the survival of the fittest and natural selection.

However, as creationists, we cannot think in this evolutionary pattern and must approach the problem in some other way. Part of your question attests to the dilemma of not being able to reconcile carnivorous dinosaurs with God's creation. But I must tell you, it isn't necessary to believe that God created vicious meat-eating dinosaurs. I am reminded of the question – Why did God create the devil? We might answer in the following manner:

Actually, God created Lucifer the "light-bearer" and Lucifer became the devil through pride and insubordination (See Isaiah 14:12-14. Also, Ezekiel 28:12-19 – Ezekiel's commentary on the life of Satan, his perfect creation, fall into evil, and final destiny in doomsday). Satan's nature was altered through sin and his glorious light was blotted out by the shameful state of evil. God was not responsible for creating a devil any more than a mother would be responsible for bringing an innocent babe into the world, only to discover later that her son has become a hardened criminal. God created dinosaurs on the sixth day and they were a part of the creation that God pronounced "very good" but, by the entrance of sin into the world, they acquired killing characteristics.

You say, "I don't think there is any evidence there were carnivorous dinosaurs. Is it correct to assume the fossil record proves that dinosaurs were vegetarians?"

It is difficult to establish proofs from the paleontological record concerning how animals acted biologically. But there are definite clues that can help establish ideas and concepts about dinosaur life styles. **The fossil record certainly indicates *there were carnivorous as well as herbivorous dinosaurs.***

We *can deduce* that the forelimbs and the three long claws of *Deinonychus* were for grasping and holding down prey, that the 70 sharp backward slanted teeth were hardly the teeth of a vegetarian, and that its powerful jaws were characteristic of a meat-eater. But these are *deductions* **that we have formulated in our mind** and *not necessarily proofs* that *Deinonychus* was, in fact, a meat-eater.

Apart from deductions we can form about dinosaurs, in regards to their meat-eating characteristics, ***allow me to give some definite evidences there were carnivorous dinosaurs. I will mention three dinosaurs from the fossil record,*** **which stand out in my mind as explicit verification these three creatures,** *were meat-eaters*:

1) *Apatosaurus* was a massive vegetarian dinosaur of about 76 feet. On the other hand, *Allosaurus* was one of the giant killers of the dinosaur world. It was about 40 feet long. How do we know, for a certainty, that *Allosaurus* was a carnivore? – **The tail bones of an *Apatosaurus*, found in one location, showed grooves from *teeth marks exactly matching teeth in the jaw of an Allosaurus* found buried with it.** Some loose teeth of the predator were also lying around. There had been a vicious fight previous to their deaths. *Apatosaurus*, in order to protect itself, swung its tail at Allosaurus and had *bite marks on some of its tailbones*. This example can serve as indicating a predator in search of a victim.

2) There is evidence that the streamlined ***Coelophysis* was a carnivore.** *Coelophysis* skeletons were found in a mass burial at Ghost Ranch, New Mexico, in 1947. Literally, dozens of skeletons were discovered all lying across one another. It is one of the most amazing dinosaur graveyards, which, I believe, was the result of *the biblical Flood*. Some of the skeletons reveal the **presence of small *Coelophysis* skeletons inside the rib cage of adult animals.** These skeletons were not babies ready to be born. All dinosaurs seem to have laid eggs but if these skeletons were believed to be the embryos within eggs, they are too large and well formed. **The gruesome fact is this: the small skeletons must therefore *represent the last meal of the adult Coelophysis*.**This is an *example of cannibalism* and reflects the fact that *Coelophysis* adults would tend *to eat any small creatures* (according to its teeth and speed) and that they would catch even their own kind.

3) My final example of a meat-eater is the familiar ***Tyrannosaurus rex***, which means the "Tyrant Lizard King." Paleontologist Robert Bakker described this dinosaur as the "10,000 pound roadrunner from hell." I have already talked about deduction. Scientists have deduced that *Tyrannosaurus* was a killing machine, which made bloodthirsty attacks on helpless prey. Paleontologists have made their deductions based on the teeth of *T.rex*, which have been called "Lethal Bananas." *Tyrannosaurus* had a massive head, which was 5 feet long, and single teeth measuring up to 7 inches long, the size of a butcher's heavy, chopping knife. It was no small wonder this dinosaur was considered to be carnivorous! **But again, this was *pure speculation. That is, until 1992.***

Kenneth H. Olson, a Lutheran pastor and fossil collector found two important specimens – *a partial pelvis from an adult Triceratops and a toe bone from an adult Edmontosaurus* (duck-billed dinosaur). Both these dinosaurs were vegetarians and both bones were *riddled with gouges and punctures up to 12 centimeters long and several centimeters deep.* The *Triceratops* had close to 80 indentations. Tests, with dental putty, were made on the fossil specimens. The evidence pointed to the indentations being *the first definitive bite marks from a T. rex.* I personally believe Olson has established a pattern of the biological behavior of *T. rex. Tyrannosaurus rex* fed upon its two most common contemporaries, *Triceratops* and *Edmontosaurus*.

You might want to add this information: The discoveries of Karen Chin in 1997. She studied a ***T. Rex Coprolite*** that was filled with pulverized bone. Chin, by using histological methods, concludes that **the crushed bone came from a *juvenile herbivorous dinosaur.*** The *T. rex* did ingest bone and partially digested the material, with strong enzymes from its stomach acids.

When some creationists attempt to set forth the idea that *T. rex was strictly a watermelon* eater, *is it any wonder that they open themselves to ridicule.* The evidence for meat-eating dinosaurs having once roamed the earth, *if not conclusive, is more that substantial.*

Tonight, we have been shown that *dinosaurs could be bitten, swallowed, and ingested by meat-eaters. In what other way can the eating process of carnivorous dinosaurs be described*? However, most every creationist realizes carnivorous dinosaurs were not a part of God's plan for His original creation (See Genesis 1:30; Isaiah 11: 6-9, 65:25).

QUESTION TWENTY-SIX:

IF IT IS TRUE THAT THERE IS EVIDENCE FOR MEAT-EATING DINOSAURS, THEN WHY DID GOD CREATE SUCH HORRIFIC CREATURES AND BRING FORTH SUCH KILLERS INTO THE ANIMAL KINGDOM?

ANSWER:

[This question came up during the course of meetings but is more personalized for this book. I thought it should follow on the heels of question twenty-five, both for over-all logic and clarification]

God made dinosaurs on the sixth day and they were a part of the creation that God pronounced "very good." However, many animals – including dinosaurs – had their natures changed following the entrance of sin into the world. How these changes came about in dinosaurs is, of course, a matter of conjecture. The development of predatory characteristics in dinosaurs could be understood from at least three possible perspectives:

1) The killing characteristics of predatory dinosaurs developed naturally through genetic alterations and mutational changes. The characteristics simply arose through evolutionary variation without limitation.

2) The killing characteristics of rapacious dinosaurs developed through the power of Satan. Through alterations within the genetic pool of certain species of dinosaurs, predatory characteristics developed. All this was done to bring reproach upon the Creator and to discredit the works of His hands – the world of nature.

3) The killing characteristics of predatory dinosaurs had developed through the power of God. They were a result of His creative omnipotence.

There may be other alternatives to consider but the above perspectives would be among the main possibilities.

Concerning the possibilities, creationists might reason in the following manner:

Possibility One: This option is contrary to the creationistic belief that variation has limitation and the Creator has placed all animals within fixed boundaries of the "kind." Darwin's theory of one type of organism being transformed into another type of organism will always remain a theory and never will become one of nature's fixed laws. God, creating rich diversity within "kinds" of animals, is not the same thing as Darwin's evolution. The idea of survival of the fittest does not contain within it any proof of a mechanistic force, which would bring about more complex animals from simpler forms.

Possibility Two: This option is probably the strongest in the thinking of most creationists. Satan manipulated gene pools in order to bring about the killing traits in dinosaurs. However, there are creationists who would take issue since they find it impossible to accept the notion that forces of evil could bring about genetic alterations within the dinosaur species or, for that matter, within any animal species. They also fear that should Satan have been granted such power, he would nearly be on the same level with God. And especially since genetic modification is somewhat creative in scope and Satan does not have the power to devise, imagine, or manufacture origins. Perhaps, a better way of looking at this issue would be to think of Satan somehow altering the nature of dinosaurs and having them use their characteristics for uses other than for what they were originally intended. For example, the teeth in predatory dinosaurs that once were used as tools for foraging and chewing vegetation would now be used for tearing and chewing animal flesh.

Possibility Three: This choice is unthinkable to most creationists. If God created dinosaurs with the intention of having them become predatory in nature and design, then it might be concluded: He actually took part in sin's fruition – death and destruction. Such meat eating constructions would controvert the Creator's nature of love and benevolence.

Of the above possibilities for explaining predatory characteristics, the second choice – with some modification – would seem to be the best choice. Satan, rather than having the power to modify gene pools, somehow changed the nature of dinosaurs. The inception of sin brought about changes in the entire natural world. Paul writes, "For the creature was made subject to vanity, *not willingly* …" (Romans 8:20 KJV). The original language (Greek) of this verse reads, "For the creation was brought down *through imperfection*." Paul, in verse 21, writes of God's creation being delivered from the bondage of corruption and imperfection. And in verse 22, the apostle mentions, "that the whole creation groaneth and travaileth in pain together …"

The main point of Paul's passage makes it clear that animals are also subject to corruption and imperfection – not just mankind. Since there was no death in the animal kingdom before the fall, there were no flesh-eating animals. According to Genesis 1:30, the original diet of all animal life was "every green plant." But the ecosystem became filled with carnivorous dinosaurs. The nature of some dinosaurs was bent towards killing and destruction and the animals no longer lived together in peace and harmony.

The Bible's description of the new earth informs men that death in the animal realm will no longer prevail. Death was and is an intruder in this world but it will have no place in God's coming kingdom. The nature of animals will be transformed to God's original plan. Their natures will be similar to their temperament before the fall. The old ecological cycle of life and death will be replaced by the linear progression of only endless existence (Younker).

In the book of Isaiah, there is a description of the nature of the animal kingdom in a sinless world that will be ushered in when all things are made new:

"The wolf will live with the lamb, the leopard will lie down with the goat, the calf and the lion and the yearling together; and a little child shall lead them. The cow will feed with the bear, their young will lie down together, and the lion will eat straw like the ox. The infant will play near the hole of the cobra, and the young child put his hand into the viper's nest. They will neither harm nor destroy on my holy mountain, for the earth will be full of the knowledge of the Lord as the waters cover the sea."

Isaiah 11:6-9

NIV

"The wolf and the lamb will feed together, and the lion will eat straw like the ox, but dust will be the serpent's food. They will neither harm nor destroy on all my holy mountain" says the LORD.

Isaiah 65:25

NIV

The prophet describes nature changed by the power of God. God's ecology, with animals living in perfect tranquility and ideal peace, challenge mankind's present understanding of ecological laws and tenets. Again, God was not responsible for bringing meat-eating dinosaurs into the animal realm. All animals were originally vegetarians but Satan altered their natures and they became brutal and unrestrained killers. In the new earth, animals will be liberated from Satan's control and, once again, enjoy benevolent and amiable natures under God's reign.

QUESTION TWENTY-SEVEN:

THE OTHER NIGHT YOU SAID THAT SATAN WAS RESPOSIBLE FOR THE KILLING CHARACTERISTICS OF DINOSAURS. I HAVE READ ABOUT THE DEFENSE PATTERNS IN CERTAIN DINOSAURS THAT WERE USED FOR PROTECTION AGAINST PREDATORS. DO YOU BELIEVE GOD CREATED THESE PROTECTIVE PATTERNS?

ANSWER:

[I responded in this manner: "First of all, in regards to your question from the 'DINOSAUR QUESTION BOX', I have spent hours in writing out notes. Having come up with different answers, I will give you the answer, which I estimate to be the best one. The audience turned in a host of questions and I apologize for not being able to answer all of them. You understand that my comments have been mostly speculative and yet I have given to you the best possible explanations from my creationist viewpoint. My answer will take the entire ten minutes of allotted time for our 'question and answer period.'" The following are a portion of my remarks rewritten in book form for my readers]

At one point in my life I did believe God, through genetic alterations, brought about defense characteristics in order to give herbivorous dinosaurs an opportunity to survive in the world of tooth-and-claw. However, the idea that Satan caused predatory characteristics in dinosaurs, through genetic intervention, sets up a rather ludicrous picture. One can imagine God and Satan sitting at the chessboard of ecology and engaging in the following conversation:

Satan (The Prince of Darkness) – "I think I will place a serration design on the teeth of some of the dinosaurs and curve their teeth backwards in order to make them more efficient killing machines. *T. Rex* will be part of my art work."

God (The Elohim of Creation) – "Carefully, watch this move! With a little genetic engineering, I will give *Triceratops* a tough hide for defense against your T. rex's steak-knife teeth and three horns to slice open T. rex's under-belly. What do you think of that?"

Satan (The Roaring Lion Who Walks on Earth) – "This act is very impressive! Because you know genetics, note this move and observe how adept I am in mutational-manipulation. Take a look at this large, curved, scythe-like claw I just placed on the second toe of the foot of this particular dinosaur. [Presently named *Deinonychus* –

"terrible claw"] This big claw will be used to attack other dinosaurs. Their bellies will be sliced open and this genetic-creation of mine will eat the entrails."

God (The Jehovah of Judgment) – "What else would I expect from you but I can easily counteract your move. I will alter the gene pool and variations will eventually produce extra large dinosaurs. They will be called sauropods and will be able to lift up their forelimbs and then come back down with crushing blows to your dinosaur. After that, your creature will starve to death due to his inability to seek out prey."

No need for me to continue with this imaginary conversation. I have made my point. If God and the devil are viewed as constantly engaged in bringing about changes in the dinosaur species, this entire picture is relegated to an absurdity. Imagine! – Dinosaurs becoming chess pieces in the hands of both God and Lucifer. The devil brings in one genetic alteration and God counter-attacks with another. Just how far can one go in assessing where God left off and the devil began or visa versa? [Special Note: God never argued with the devil (Jude, verse nine) but He did have conversations with him (Job 1:6-12; Luke 4:1-14, etc.)]

Creationists should take a dim view of such a notion as two forces – good and evil – manipulating the dinosaurian species like pawns upon the Mesozoic chessboard. Rather than God crafting defense attributes through genetic changes that would entail constant improvising to counteract carnivore attacks, *God could have used herbivorous dinosaur features already in place at creation.* For examples: **The *large tails* of the giant sauropod dinosaurs,** used for balancing their long-necked bodies, could also have been used as weapons, which were thrown around in a circular motion towards predatory enemies. Such force would induce injury and possible death to opponents.

The *three horns* of *Triceratops* used for foraging vegetation and digging up tough rooted plants, could have been used as formidable weaponry. The horns are considered to be the most dangerous devices for active defense among the dinosauria. Thus, it can be understood that the horns of *Triceratops* would not only have been used for the primary purpose of foraging plants but the additional purpose of active defense weapons. Such an adaptation could have been developed almost immediately because of Triceratops's instinctive will for personal survival. These two examples should suffice for dinosaur characteristics being used for more than a singular purpose.

These will be my closing thoughts for this evening: God did not permit terror to have full sway over His creation. He did not allow Satan to have total charge over his creatures. God gave the weaker and less ferocious dinosaurs a fighting chance to maintain their lives. Defenses aided dinosaurs in resisting the pain and suffering, which the prince of hate sought to inflict upon them. A compassionate God made it possible for the life of peaceful dinosaurs to continue a little longer on this earth. He gave these animals a fighting chance to preserve their lives over and against the power of Satan's hatred. **The docile dinosaurs, because of the implanted will to survive, took whatever necessary apparatus (even the voice, as in QUESTION THIRTY-ONE, could be used to warn other dinosaurs or as a fright tactic to scare predators; not to mention the fancy armor with spikes and incredible, protective coating which featured thick plates) God had fashioned for peaceful existence in their environment and used them as means of defense and weapons for survival.**

QUESTION TWENTY-EIGHT:

WHY HAVE NO DINOSAUR BONES BEEN FOUND AT THE LA BREA TAR PITS?

ANSWER:

[This question was placed in the DINOSAUR QUESTION BOX and is a common one, especially here in California]

This is an accurate fact. At the museum, there are dinosaur movies, tapes, puzzles, coloring books, models, trinkets, drinking glasses and even a dinosaur theatre **but *no* dinosaur bones have ever been discovered at the tar pits. Why is this true?**

An **evolutionist** could easily answer this question by saying, "The animals that were found in the tar pits are ice age animals. The Pleistocene sediments containing such creatures go back in time to only about 1.8 million years. On the other hand, dinosaurs were annihilated 65 million years ago. The reason dinosaur bones were not discovered with dire wolves, saber-toothed tigers, mammoths, and giant, ground sloths, etc., is because the dinosaur had been extinct for over 63 million years." **The creationist**, like I am, might say, "The dinosaur did not live in the same ecological niche as did the animals discovered in tar. The dinosaurs escaped entrapment because they lived elsewhere." The Noachian Flood destroyed the majority of them; many more died out after their release from the ark and following the Ararat migration, due to natural causes.

The remnant of dinosaurs died, as did many other animal kinds, which could not survive the Ice Age and, therefore, became extinct. There have been a few dinosaurs discovered in southern California but none of them have been found in tar pits. There are other creationists, I not included, who not only believe that dinosaurs survived the Ice Age but sauropods still have existence. I will speak to this assumption in the next question – TWENTY-NINE.

MYTHS

QUESTION TWENTY- NINE:

ARE DINOSAURS LIVING TODAY?

ANSWER:

[This is purely a *book question* designed with the hope of giving readers a more realistic approach to the subject of dinosaurs and to be able to recognize a myth or fairy tale from what is real and factual]

The book, *Reader's Digest Mysteries of the Unexplained*, "reports … something weird in central Africa rivers and swamps going back to the 1800's."

P.150

Many creationists are convinced of the existence of the legendary monster known as *Mokele-Mbembe* (mo-KE-le-MEM-be). This is the "something weird" reported by Congo pygmies as half-elephant, half-dragon. On the basis of eyewitness reports, a number of investigatory expeditions have been sent into the "dark jungles" and "trackless swamps" of the African Congo. "Dark jungles" and "trackless swamps" are the ways writers love to describe Africa. But Africa is no longer the DARK CONTINENT where WEIRD ANIMALS are likely to be discovered, for example – sauropods (Jacobs).

I have books of maps and geographical descriptions of Africa. It does not appear to me, any dark areas are left in Africa. The geographers of that continent have done a much better job at revealing land and water entities than cryptozoologists have done in discovering dinosaurs.

This monster – *Mokele-Mbembe* – has been described in the following ways (*Reader's Digest Mysteries of the Unexplained*, P.150; *Quest for the African Dinosaurs*, P.245) :

1) Ferman Mosomele, when he was 14 years old, saw a reddish-brown, snakelike head and neck six to eight feet long. When shown a book of animal pictures, he picked a sauropod dinosaur (Definition of a sauropod: An immense four-legged plant-eater with small, bulky body, and long neck and tail).

2) A man named Appolonaire sketched for one of the expeditions, a picture in the soil that is said to resemble a sauropod. [But pictures and sketches should not be counted as substantial evidence in conforming the living, actuality of dinosaurs – especially when there is not the least bit of empirical confirmation to back up their existence]

3) A woman saw two beasts killed by villagers on Lake Tele. They had cut up the monsters and eaten them. [These villagers must have been awfully hungry to hack up approximately 64 feet of dinosaur meat. Did the women see the lake people eat the sauropods in one sitting?]

4) A young girl could not tell the neck from the tail of the animal and described the body to be the size of four elephants. She and her parents allegedly found prints of this animal.

5) Nicolas Mondongo described the animal as 32 feet long and topped with a cockscomb. [A cockscomb is pretentious head attire much like that seen on a rooster. This description was supposed to give the monster a dragon-like appearance]

With all the reported sightings and verbal attestations to allegedly confirm the existence of sauropods; the chances of very large and striking land animals eluding human exploration for more than a century and a half, in my opinion, is next to inconceivable.

Cryptozoology is a true science that pertains to the study of animals, which live in dark and hidden places. A number of weird and mysterious animals have been discovered. For examples: The giant forest hog discovered in the twentieth century; the first live okapi captured in 1903. This creature was a short-necked giraffe and its lower legs had stripes like a zebra. The *Coelacanth* was caught off the coast of South Africa and supposed to have been extinct for 80 million years. The existence of the above animals has been well documented and their reality has been confirmed. This is more than we can say for the avowed, living presence of sauropods.

Cryptozoology apparently does find new and unidentified animals and even animals from the remote past, "unknown" animals become "known." A fossil from the past is found in a presently, living creature. However, there are times when a find proves to be something else rather than what scientists first thought it to be. For instance: the smelly monster found by the Japanese fishing boat *Zuiyo Maru*, near New Zealand in 1977. The fisherman measured it to be 32 feet long, photographed it, and even took tissue samples. They threw it overboard so it would not contaminate the fish they had already netted. Some Scientists claimed that this "monster" was none other than a *Plesiosaur ("near lizard")*. [Mary Anning of Britain discovered one of the earliest fossils of a Plesiosaur when she was only twelve years old. *Plesiosaurs* were giant reptiles of the Jurassic seas judged by evolutionists to be about 150 million years ago]. The tissue samples that were taken from this partly decomposed creature indicate that the animal was a *basking shark*. When sharks decay, they form a pattern, which *superficially resembles a plesiosaur* (See P. Jerlstrom and B. Elliott, "Let Rotting Sharks Lie: Further evidence for Shark Identity of the Zuiyo-maru Carcass," CEN *Technical Journal* 13(2): 83-87, 1999).

Some creationists still publish in many of their books, a photograph of this so-called *Plesiosaur*. I have seen this picture numerous times and many of my fellow creationists claim that this establishes the fact: *Plesiosaurs* are still living. The *Plesiosaur* carcass netted by this Japanese trawler was estimated to have been dead for about a month. Therefore, claim certain creationists, the discovery of this marine reptile proved that the earth was young and not the millions and billions of years as claimed by evolutionists. I believe in a young earth but this *Plesiosaur* (?) is not what it was once thought to be. Thus, it can no longer serve as a testimony to a young earth. This is a case, a rotting shark carcass is not indicative of a true cryptozoological specimen.

As we once more return to *Mokele-mbembe*, I must make known my skepticism. It seems to me this science – cryptozoology – often branches off into pure science fiction. Since dinosaurs have been extinct for over 3,950 years (at least from the time of the Ice Age) it is highly doubtful there are any living specimens that survived to this present day and time – especially sauropods that were giants and the largest land animals of all time. Until proved otherwise, NO DINOSAURS LIVE IN AFRICA. Those who accept Mokele-mbembe as a living dinosaur may be accepting folklore in place of true science.

Let us consider the following facts: Sauropods were herding animals and it is unlikely that such an animal would be discovered alone. Alleged sightings have been reported for almost two hundred years and only on Lake Tele. A woman *reported*: *villagers had eaten more than one "monster"*. Does the report of more than one sauropod imply that there have been offspring? Does the sauropod have a mate? If so, over the space of two hundred years, it would seem that there was more than enough time for reproduction.

If there were a productive female sauropod, then she would have laid eggs in a clutch and arranged the eggs in an orderly fashion. Where are her nesting sites over the past two hundred years? With the possibility of reproduction generating families of sauropods, should there not be more sightings by natives of Africa? Again, it is highly unlikely that such giants could have survived to this present day and if they did, there definitely should be more evidence of nesting sites. With the possibility of dinosaur hatchlings, why is there no evidence of eggshells or complete eggs, which still contain embryos – either living or dead?

Dinosaurologists have discovered coprolites (fossilized dung) of extinct dinosaurs. Is it not strange that, with the belief in present living dinosaurs, no huge piles of giant sauropod excrement have ever been discovered in the jungles or plains of Africa? Or is such an item beneath the dignity of the thought processes of men who continue to search with the romantic notion of finding dinosaurs?

In fact, there has been no visible evidence of a sauropod except for the alleged discovery of footprints by a young girl and her parents. What happened? Did jungle vegetation grow over the footprints before the cryptologists arrived at the scene? Why not the detection of other footprints since the dinosaur is alleged to have present day existence? Would not huge footprints be discovered somewhere in the plains of Africa or do these animals choose to hide out only in vegetation, which soon covers their trackways? Did the young girl and her parents have the misfortune of discovering only one footprint and not several? Did nature's flooring have the softness to record only one footprint or did it have the pliability to record a trackway series? If it does have the impressionability of recording tracks, then where are such tracks? Obviously, they exist only in man's imagination.

Why not the discovery of gizzard stones, which are highly polished, and belched up by sauropods? Sauropods were plant eaters and they constantly made use of such stones, which aided digestion by grinding tough plant food. Living sauropods ate hundreds of tons of vegetation each day. Have there been any foraging sights discovered? In other words, have there been any remnants or evidences of sauropods living in Africa that can serve as additional evidence and be included in with the mysterious and supernatural appearances of such creatures?

Extinct sauropod species vary in length from 60 feet to 100 feet and, sometimes, much larger. If the present sightings are true and sauropods are of similar size, then the "African dinosaur" has no natural enemies. Even "kings of the jungle," whether they are lions or pachyderms, wouldn't dare to confront or squabble with a Giant Sauropod. It is not exactly like a sauropod needs to hide or camouflage itself. Who or what thing could the animal possibly fears? If it exits at all, then it should be readily seen. Helicopters ought to be flown over the densest fauna to see if a sauropod is foraging. Since it lifts its head above the treetops as it eats, it should be caught in the act of consuming vegetation. A sauropod must continually eat since it devours over 300 tons of vegetation each day. Surely, a Helicopter could easily spot a sauropod.

With the starvation and health deficiencies throughout the continent of Africa, it is a source of wonder to me that men can spend time and money in hunting for the alleged extant sauropod. But I understand that such men hold religious services and sing hymns with natives, who help them search for the elusive and imaginatory vegetarian beast. I suppose there is some satisfaction to be gained and the contentment that grows out of such meetings is more than enough to appease the inward conscience of that man who is on a quest for living, African dinosaurs.

The following quote is from the book, *The Counter-Creationism*, by Mark Isaak, P.100:

O'Hanlon (1997, 373) reported the answer upon asking a native if he had seen *Mokele-mbembe:*

"What a stupid question," said Doubla, looking genuinely surprised. "Mokele-mbembe is not an animal like a gorilla or python. And Mokele-mbembe is not a sacred animal. It doesn't appear to people. It is an animal of mystery. It exists because we imagine it. But to see it – never. You don't see it."

I would suppose that a belief system concerning *Mokele-mbembe* could be built on whomever the Congo native happens to be in giving out information at the time of inquiry.

When it comes to *Mokele-mbembe* of the Congo, Loch Ness monster of Scotland, The Devil's Hoof Marks of Devon, England; hairy, wild men, footprints of the Himalayas, Sasquatch of Bluff Creek Valley in northern California, etc., are all good reasons for me, in my refusal, to take some creationists as serious students of science. Cryptozoology has its place but too often has led creationists to skip down the pathway of life with a merry, care-free, and happy-go-lucky attitude as they whistle the tune: "Science is to believe anything so long as everything is believable."

QUESTION THIRTY:

ARE THE DRAGONS MENTIONED IN THE BIBLE, DINOSAURS?

ANSWER:

[This is a book question. Fanciful notions and spurious concepts have been attached to biblical interpretation throughout the course of history. The equation that identifies the dragons of the Bible to be none other than dinosaurs of natural history is a bogus claim. The reason I regard this identification to be perilous: if scholars of biblical studies are satisfied with such shallow rules for Bible exegesis, then exegesis (when it comes to the major doctrines of the Bible) will be transformed from the science of interpretation to the mere speculations of human philosophy. Theology will be a thing of the past. The "sure word of prophecy" will be exchanged for the uncertain claims of human speculation]

In the King James Version of the Bible; *dragon* or *large serpent* is mentioned 13 times in the New Testament (all in the book of Revelation) and 6 times in the Old Testament. *Dragons* or *serpents are* mentioned 16 times in the Old Testament.

Thus, *dragon* (*serpent*) and the plural *dragons* (*serpents*) have a total of 35 combined references in the Bible.

Many creationists believe, in every case, these 35 texts indicate "dinosaur" or "dinosaurs."

These same creationists are quick to point out the name "dinosaur" did not originate until the ninetieth century and the book of Job, for example, mentions dragons (serpents) thirty-five hundred years ago. But they contend that dragons (serpents) are referring to the same kind of animal. [For more information on the origin of the name "dinosaurs," my readers may want to review QUESTION TWENTY]

The only way to check out creationist teachers on the veracity of their theory (Dragons equal Dinosaurs) is to check a number of the biblical references of dragon (serpent) and dragons (serpents) IN CONTEXT. That is, when are the words understood to be symbolical, mythological, poetical, or historical and literal?

Let's begin with the word *dragons* (serpents) in the Old Testament:

*DEUTERONOMY 32:24 KJV – ".... I will also send the teeth of beasts upon them, with the poison of serpents (dragons) of the dust."

This section of scripture is entitled the *Song of Moses*. God will bring *curses* against Israel for their disobedience. The *blessing* was seen in God's protection of Israel, while they were in the wilderness, against "fiery serpents." This, in context, was a literal but conditional act of God involving poisonous snakes or vipers – NOT DINOSAURS. Serpents are often described as creatures "of the dust" – NOT DINOSAURS.

*JOB 30:29 KJV – "I am brother to dragons, and a companion to owls."

In this case, Job is bewailing his present humiliation as Satan strikes him down with disease. Micah uses the same imagery of himself in **MICAH 1:8 KJV** – "… I will make a wailing like the dragons and mourning as the owls." In both references, **"jackals"** is used by the NIV in place of **"dragons"** of the KJV. In the Hebrew language, as is quite often the case, a certain word has to be translated according to the local context and especially when it comes to animals. But those creationists, who admittedly are advanced Hebrew scholars, do not like the word "jackals." They think the Hebrew word, going back 3500 years ago, should always be translated "dragons," which in modern terminology means "dinosaurs."

Job felt alone and without God or true friends. He felt like the jackals and owls that would frequent the ruins of abandoned cities and would wail as do jackals and give the strange mourning sound like owls. This is a sight seen in this present day and time. In the first place, by the time of Job, dinosaurs had been extinct for almost 150 years.

In the second place, dinosaurs did not hang around abandoned cities and wail in accompaniment with owls. What a strange and silly notion! "Jackals" is a better translation – NOT "DINOSAURS." Dinosaurs do not fit the context. Job and Micah were simply using imagery to describe their personal feelings. They both, in their suffering, wailed like the jackal and mourned like the owls.

*PSALMS 74:12-14 KJV – "For God is my King of old, working salvation in the midst of the earth. Thou didst divide the sea by thy strength: thou break the heads of the dragons in the waters. Thou break the heads of leviathan in pieces, and gavest him to be meat to the people inhabiting the wilderness."

This portion of scripture, of course, recalls the mighty acts of God as Creator, King, and Savior, when he delivered his people from Egypt. God opened up the Red Sea and destroyed the Egyptians and their chariots. I suppose that many creationists would translate "Tanninum" (dragons) as *dinosaurs*. "Thou break the heads of the dragons in the waters." In the first place, there is no such animal as a dinosaur with *more than one head*.

In the second place, this is *imagery borrowed from Near Eastern creation myths*. The creator-god overcame the many-headed monster of the primeval chaotic waters before setting up the world order.

In the third place, this is highly, poetical language used to depict God's deliverance of his people from the Egyptians that were pursuing them through the Red Sea, NOT GOD'S VICTORY OVER DINOSAURS.

*MALACHI 1:3 – "And I hated Esau, and laid his mountains and his heritage waste for the dragons of the wilderness."

[The reader is referred to QUESTIONS SIXTEEN AND SEVENTEEN and the last three paragraphs]

I will present one more example from the book of Revelation:

*REVELATION 12:3,9; 13:4 – "And there appeared another wonder in heaven; and behold a great red dragon …and the great dragon was cast out, that old serpent, called the Devil, and Satan which deceiveth the whole world and they worshipped the dragon."

The Modern Creation Trilogy: Scripture and Creation by Henry M. Morris and John D. Morris are, for the most part, informative. But the section on page 207 in volume 1, entitled *Dragons in Paradise*, is neither instructive nor enlightening. I can well agree with the two creationists who point out, dinosaur mania is taking hold of the youth of the world and the interest in dinosaurs is fast becoming a public issue for propagating evolutionary propaganda.

I can well understand how Revelation twelve and thirteen is given a futuristic spin by some creationists – it is a part of their doctrine … "In the Bible's great prophecy concerning the humanistic dictator who will reign over the world for a brief time at the end of the age, a man appropriately called the Beast will arise, who will not 'regard any god,' but will only 'honor the god of forces' (Dan.11: 37-38). We read that 'all the world wondered after the beast. And they worshipped the dragon which gave power unto the beast (Rev. 13-3-4).'"

[Ibid. P.210]

On the other hand, they should be aware of the fact: not all creationists who reject Darwin's doctrine of Evolution accept Darby's doctrine of Literalism. I choose to be among the millions of creationists who remain true to the Protestant reformers and their contextual, historical method for interpreting Bible prophecy. The part I fail to understand: the application of the prophecy of Revelation 12:3, 9; 13:4 to dinosaur mania. Is this the "Bible's great prophecy"? Is this particular blend of creationists merely using the *flavor of scripture* in their portrayal of the *dragon being identified with a dinosaur* or **do they actually believe this method of analyzing Bible texts to be the proper way of interpreting Scripture**?

The **dragon** of Revelation 12 and 13 **is easily identified!** It primarily stands as a symbol for Satan but it also stands for pagan Rome that was ruling in the days when Christ was born. Satan, working through pagan Rome, had sought to destroy the "man child" who was none other than the Lord Jesus Christ. Satan used Herod (the representative of the Roman power) who attempted to destroy Christ at His birth. Rome was the only earthly government who could be symbolized in this prophecy; its dominion was universal. People who have studied history know that next to the eagle, the dragon was painted red and appeared on the principal standard of the Roman legions. **The dragon stood for pagan Rome – NOT A DINOSAUR. The prophecies of Revelation include a local application and it had nothing to do with dinosaurs.** [Special Note: The dragon painted on the Roman standards stood for pagan Rome. *The origin* of the *dragon image* being a part of various cultures and nations of the earth that I believe sprang from the observation of fossilized dinosaurs, is quite *another issue* altogether but this does not make dinosaurs the subject of Revelation 12 and 13. This "other issue" is mentioned in QUESTION 13]

The above examples are indicative of the problem in attempting to substitute "dinosaurs" for "dragons" in the King James Version. Not only do I disagree with many of my fellow creationists in their conclusion that "dragon," in every instance, should be translated dinosaur but *I haven't found one example in all 35 texts, wherein this language-formula or literary- substitution proves to be true.* **In every passage, one can discover the absurdities of this form of Bible study. I am convinced that** *any study of the Scriptures must include a regard for contextual consideration.*

QUESTION THIRTY-ONE:

DID DINOSAURS BREATH FIRE?

ANSWER:

Just this last week, I spoke with two of my professional friends about dinosaurs breathing fire. One of them laughed out loud and the other said, "No wonder, scientists don't take you guys seriously." "You guys," meaning creationists. I thought about what he said and determined to get to the bottom of this issue. It is a sad thing for me as I realize that the very best scholars of creationism acknowledge as true science, a story right out of the 168 Hans Christian Andersen's fairy tales. I cannot pass over such an interpretation of the Bible passage – **Job 41:18-21** – that concludes dinosaurs breathed fire, **without offering another viewpoint.**

In the book, *Duane T. Gish gives in Dinosaurs by Design an excellent description of the bombardier beetle* on pages 82-83. This beetle can be a problem for evolutionists because of its ability to mix chemicals and shoot out hot gasses at its enemies. Such an apparatus is difficult to explain by genetic mutations. But this description comes immediately after comments on Job 41:18-21 by Gish, who describes *leviathan* **as the dinosaur** *Parasaurolophus.* I realize that Duane Gish is *the prince of creationists* and after reading just about everything written by him, almost stand in total agreement with him. **But when he equates the legendary creature,** *leviathan* **with the fossilized and historical dinosaur,** *Parasaurolophus***, I part company with him and other creationists who adhere to the same belief.** At the foot of his comments, a beautiful, colored illustration stands out in all its vividness and **depicts** *Parasaurolophus* **breathing fire against a meat-eating predator.**

I am not aware *Parasaurolophus* is one of the few dinosaurs without a means of defense, since **the ability to make loud noises is considered to be a good asset for protection.** But to deduce a fire-breathing devise, I believe, is going too far out on the limb of imagination. Frankly, I am surprised at the *comparison between a tiny beetle and a 5-ton dinosaur*. Not only is it a long jump between the two creatures in their physical appearance but also a long jump in the biological apparatus that would enable a dinosaur to breath fire. **Gish makes no mention of protecting the mouth and throat of dinosaurs perceived as breathing fire.**

In all the books I have read concerning *Parasaurolophus,* never has this creature been associated with the sea. It has been linked with a *terrestrial form of life.* Job and chapter 41 speak about *leviathan* as a sea creature. Also, is it an aspect of true science to associate a mythical and legendary sea creature with the literal and historical land dinosaur, *Parasaurolophus*? *Leviathan* is defined as "one spirally wound" which, I am sure, **does not sound like nor is a true biological characteristic.** "Covered with scales" is quite possible for a sea creature but to "make the sea to boil like a pot" would be a physical impossibility even though it is described as breathing fire and smoke. ***Leviathan is an imaginary sea monster borrowed by the prophets of Israel from the Ugaritic Texts. Such a monster symbolized the powers of the world that afflicted God's people.***

If we believe that *leviathan* of Job 41 was a literal creature that breathed fire and smoke, then we might also believe that the *leviathan* mentioned in Job 3:8 was *able to swallow the day and night of Job's birth*. If my fellow-creationists become so inclined to believe symbolic and figurative language can be used to describe literal fire-breathing dinosaurs, then how can **they write against those creationists who fail to see the literal interpretation of the seven days of creation?**

If creationists are going to accept the literal interpretation of *leviathan* breathing smoke and fire in Job 41, then why not accept the horses with smoke and brimstone issuing "out of their mouths" – **Revelation 9:17-18** (Mark Isaac). Fire-breathing animals (snakes, bulls, horses, etc.), can be traced through the course of man's history. This is a folklore motif *not to be taken literally.* **How far must we go as creationists in establishing mythological creatures for biblical literalism?** For a people interested in historical fiction versus nonfiction, the levels of determining narrative writing from poetry; for the sake of determining the meaning of Genesis 1:1 to 2:3: it is simply amazing to me how these same people can fall flat in principles of interpretation when analyzing the literal or poetical basis for Job 41.

Gish contends, "Those hollow crests must have been used for something. Why not a method of defense?" [Ibid.P.83] I wonder if Gish is familiar with that other theory of the crest being a method of defense! **The U-tube in the *Parasaurolophus* not only looked like a trombone, it was a trombone!**

Bakker writes:

"If the duckbill inhaled or exhaled with force, the U-tube would be a resonating chamber, enriching the tone and amplifying the noise."

The Dinosaur Heresies

Robert T. Bakker

P.43

Bakker also writes:

"The most complex headgear of all among the duckbills belonged to *Parasaurolophus*. Each nostril started with a separate trombone-shaped tube leading from the nose up to the top of the skull, then out and behind the very long crest, a sharp U-turn and back down the crest, then down along the head, and through to the windpipe. Since each nostril had a complete tube of its own, a crest in section reveals four separate chambers – two ingoing and two outgoing. Hollow-crested duckbills are widely regarded – certainly with good reason – as head-hooters, amplifying and modulating their cries through their crests. All of the varied, hollow cranial ornaments were specialized outgrowths of the normal air tract."

[Ibid. P.345]

The *Parasaurolophus* attracted the opposite sex with his attractive head structure and with his ability to make a hooting noise. This made him more attractive to the female and this theory is more in keeping with the ways of God in the course of nature than the outlandish theory of fire-breathing dinosaurs. How to win a mate was part of the instinctive factors built into God's creatures. **Also, we must not forget that dinosaurs had many *defense methods*, among which was the ability to make *loud noises in warning* other members of the herd and also *in scaring* off predators.** The resonating chamber of the U-tube could readily have served for such a purpose as defense. This theory far outweighs the notion of a fire-breathing characteristic.

QUESTION THIRTY-TWO:

IS LEVIATHAN IN THE BOOK OF JOB, A DINOSAUR?

ANSWER:

[In QUESTION TWENTY and THIRTY-ONE, *Leviathan* was not considered to be a dinosaur. Please see my response to these questions. The following answer is a reply to QUESTION THIRTY-TWO and will merely be a short review of what already has been stated. This question is definitely a book one]

Duane Gish equates Leviathan with *Parasaurolophus*. Gish writes, "*Parasaurolophus* had a great bony crest with hollow chambers. Perhaps a *Parasaurolophus* could combine chemicals in his hollow crest and spray a combustible mixture, which would spontaneously ignite when contacting the oxygen in the air" (*Dinosaurs by Design*, P.82).

The "hollow crest" is much more complicated than the description given by Gish. The four separate chambers of the crest section are impossible to translate this apparatus into a suitable mechanism for combining and spraying chemicals. Gish infers this story does not sound a little farfetched when one considers the bombardier beetle. **For me, the story of the fire-breathing dinosaur** *does sound farfetched and the unlikely comparison with the beetle, confirms it.*

It is also important to remember that *Parasaurolophus* was a land animal – not a sea monster. *Leviathan* of Job 41 is not a dinosaur. The monster is linked to folklore and because of its intended symbolical meaning, is not to be taken literally. If some creationists are going to accept the literal interpretation of leviathan breathing smoke and fire in Job 41, then why not accept the horses with smoke and brimstone issuing 'out of their mouths'"? – Revelation 9:17-18 (Isaac). **In the comparison of these two texts from Job and John the revelator, the symbolic intention of these men of God should readily be perceived and duly noted.**

QUESTIONS ON DATING (DEEP TIME)

QUESTION THIRTY-THREE:

CREATIONISTS BELIEVE THAT DINOSAURS EXISTED ONLY FOR THOUSAND OF YEARS RATHER THAN MILLIONS OF YEARS. DINOSAUR TRACTS HAVE BEEN FOUND IN CERTAIN COAL DEPOSITS FORMED MILLIONS OF YEARS AGO. WOULD IT BE CORRECT TO ASSUME THAT DINOSAURS EXISTED FOR MILLIONS OF YEARS ALSO?

ANSWER:

[This was from the DINOSAUR BOX and I still consider it to be one of the finest questions ever raised in a meeting on the subject of dinosaurs. To this day, I do not know the source of the question. I have to believe that there was an evolutionist in the audience. They were always welcome and I made that fact clear. I was 38 years old when conducting my first meeting on evolution and creation. There was an evolutionist present and he was introduced to me before the meeting began. I did some silent praying and I was a little nervous but I knew the subject was God's choosing. I will never forget how gracious this evolutionist was. He did not discomfort me in any way and he saved his questions until after the meeting. We talked for about an hour]

Apparently, some people establish in their mind the following syllogism:

Major Premise: Geological time took millions of years to build up coal deposits.

Minor Premise: Dinosaur tracts have been found in coal deposits.

Conclusion: **Therefore, dinosaurs are millions of years old.**

As we assimilate the following information, let us see if we have evidence to counteract the above Major Premise. If either the Major Premise or the Minor Premise is wrong, the entire syllogism is incorrect.

The era for coal formation, in the Geological Column, is based on the belief in uniformity involving a great deal of time, but **coal seams were formed in a rather short time period and are convincing evidence for a Universal Flood.**

Geologists claim that coal beds are formed by vegetation in peat bogs, marshes, and swamps, but there are coal beds in this earth that exceed 500 feet in thickness. This is the vertical extent. The horizontal extent is even more staggering – the Appalachian coal basin that **extends over some 70,000 square miles,** serves as a good example.

On the average, it takes about 10 feet of vegetation to form a foot of coal. Since some coal beds are 500 feet in thickness, 5000 feet of vegetation was needed to form such seams. In the world today few peat bogs, swamps, or marshes reach 100 feet in depth. **How impossible it is to account for coal seams on the basis of uniformity.** The vast amounts of vegetation needed for the formation of coal have not come from vegetation grown in place. **Rather, the sources of coal have come from countless tons of vegetation washed in by tremendous volumes of water.**

Only the Noachian Flood could account for the coal seams we see today. Coal beds did not take millions of years to form and the doctrine of uniformity is totally inadequate to explain the vertical and horizontal extent of their formation and appearance in the geological strata.

Peterson describes a situation in Utah: *Dinosaurs* walking on piles of vegetable debris *left footprints that protrude into the coal from the mud above.* He writes:

"The tracks seem to have been made at a time when the peat accumulation was covered with a foot or more of mud ….The feet sank through the mud several inches, or even more that a foot at times, into soft, yielding peat underneath. In most places the coal is easily separated from the roof, leaving the track-shaped protuberance extending partly or wholly as a definite appendage from the ceiling. The largest tracks are those, which protrude farthest from the roof … The tracks … have been observed … at intervals over an area more than one hundred miles in extent and *in different seams of coal*, which represent a stratigraphic thickness of more than two hundred feet of sandstone including three or four beds of coal. The coal seams total in thickness approximately thirty-five feet."

[Peterson W., 1924 *Dinosaur tracks in the roof of coalmines.* Natural History, 24 (3): 388. (Peterson's quote is from *Creation – Accident or Design?* by Harold G. Coffin, Pp.77-78)]

An evolutionist makes the above statements. Coffin, a creationist, follows Peterson's remarks by proposing his own theory:

"**It is not reasonable to suppose** that successive bogs developed repeatedly in same location after each previous one but was buried suddenly by water-carried sediments, that similar animals played around in each of these marshes, and that these unchanging conditions continued for **several millions of years.**"

"On the other hand, it is **difficult to visualize clearly how successive levels of tracks were made by these animals under conditions of flooding.** However, there is much evidence of the rapid silting over of these vegetable deposits. **An event of relatively short duration that deposited vegetable matter and silt alternatively** while dinosaurs were wading or swimming around in the muddy water is a better theory."

Creation – Accident or Design? [Italics, mine]

P.78

The Revised & Expanded Answers Book has some apropos thoughts for our present dinosaur and coal question:

"The youngest coal is supposed to be millions of years old, and most of it is supposed to be 10s or 100s of millions of years old. Such old coal should be devoid of C-14. It isn't. No source of coal has been found that completely lacks C-14. ....

"It is an unsolved mystery to evolutionists as to why coal has C-14 in it, or wood supposedly many millions of years old still has C-14 present, but it makes perfect sense in a creationist world view."

P.87

When vegetation dies, it no longer absorbs carbon from the air. The accumulated C-14 slowly decays back to nitrogen. This means any vegetation that was used in the process of coal-making and past 75,000 years, **should no longer contain C-14.** For example, Pennsylvania coal, which if purported to be hundreds of millions of years old should no longer contain C-14 but it, does. What does this fact tell us? – Coal cannot be dated in "deep time." In other words, *coal is much younger than what is depicted in the geological time scale.* Thus, associating dinosaurs with coal seams will not afford the evolutionist with long periods of time for dinosaur existence.

In view of the above facts, it is time to rewrite our syllogism:

Major Premise: Coal deposits can be formed within a short time period – not millions of years.

Minor Premise: Dinosaur tracks have been found in coal deposits.

Conclusion: **Therefore, dinosaur tracks discovered in coal deposits were left a short time period ago and fail to prove dinosaurs to be millions of years old.**

QUESTION THIRTY-FOUR:

SO FAR, IN THESE MEETINGS, YOU HAVEN'T SAID ANYTHING ABOUT CARBON-14 AND DINOSAURS. WOULDN'T THIS TYPE OF TESTING MAKE DINOUSARS MILLIONS OF YEARS OLD RATHER THAN THOUSAND OF YEARS LIKE YOU SAID? EXPLAIN C-14 TO THE AUDIENCE.

ANSWER:

[Dinosaur meetings can never be planned without anticipating this question and other questions having to do with dating of the earth. This question will always be posited and should never be avoided by those of us who believe in a *young earth*]

Actually, evolutionists do not use carbon-14 for dating dinosaurs. They claim that dinosaurs became extinct about 65 million years ago and since carbon dating is only good up to about 75,000 years, some other dating system must be employed.

However, because carbon-14 is alleged to cover such a long period of time and since most creationists believe the earth to be only about 6-10 thousand years old, the question should be addressed. The C-14 time scale, as I said, covers a period of about 75, 000 years but some books claim 10-15,000 years and others, 30,000 years.

How reliable is C-14 testing? This is the big question. The facts indicate age discrepancies are common in this type of testing. The results of such testing should be a concern for evolutionists. For example, in Wyoming, ivory from a mammoth skeleton was tested. The carbon dating test showed an age of 11,550 years. Yet, wood in the same gravel and using the same test registered only 5,000 years. This is a major discrepancy. Yet, an example such as this one can be multiplied time and time again.

I have been asked to explain C-14. I will make it simple since I am not equipped with the knowledge capable of making it complicated. To begin, most radiocarbon specialists believe in the doctrine of uniformity and in the progressive evolutionary development of life. These beliefs are basic to their understanding of the C-14 dating method. These specialists attempt to harmonize the C-14 information with their general worldview.

But what is carbon dating? Here is the *simple explanation:*

Cosmic rays that are in the earth's atmosphere produce carbon with 14 units of mass and this carbon is distributed throughout all living material (plant and animal).

Something happens when a plant or animal dies. The process of receiving C-14, from the environment, stops. The process is terminated – ended.

What happens to the C-14 already within the plant or animal tissue? Carbon-14 is unstable. What does this mean? It means the carbon will convert back to nitrogen. Thus, over a period of time, there will be smaller amounts of C-14 and more of nitrogen in the animal tissue or plant sample.

Laboratory measurements of this conversion from carbon to nitrogen has determined that every 5,730 years, plants and animals will contain half as much radioactive carbon as they did at death. Also, **5,568 years,** has been used as an average time for conversion. This known process is set up into a time scale for plants and animals, which allegedly demonstrates the amount of time carbon converts back into nitrogen. This is basically how the carbon-14 dating system works.

This method of dating organic substances is based on a prejudicial stand against the book of Genesis (6:1— 9:17) and leads to the

FIRST ASSUMPTION (There was no Universal Flood):

But if there was a Universal Flood the following could have happened: 1) After the Flood, it would take many years to build up C-14 concentration to balance formation and decay. Since Flood action would have destroyed most of the C-14, any material buried after the Flood would show a low concentration of carbon-14. Thus, the objects when tested would appear to be much older than they really are. **2)** The Flood Catastrophe would have brought large amounts of water down to the earth from the upper atmosphere. Carbon-14 within the upper atmosphere would have been dissolved and precipitated at the Flood. What would have been the result? – A very low concentration of C-14 immediately after the Flood. Therefore, specimens of plants and animals living just before the Flood or immediately after would be dated as very old when tested by present-day concentrations.

However, rejecting the Universal Flood and accepting the Doctrine of Uniformity is not without its problems. In light of the very reasonable chance that the concentration of radiocarbon in the atmosphere had varied in the past, makes ages estimated by carbon-14 testing open to mistrust. The uniformity of C-14 concentration is only an assumption and cannot be demonstrated. The belief that the present radiocarbon concentration in the atmosphere, has continued all the way back for many thousand of years, cannot be evidenced.

There are main-line churches that accept the uniformity doctrine since carbon dating conflicts with the 6,000-year chronology of the Bible. This is due to the fact they believe C-14 testing is the last word for dating and gives the true ages of organic materials. Yet, at best, the testing may determine when an organism lived with relation to other organisms but it can never be a direct means of discovering how many solar years ago that organism actually lived.

SECOND ASSUMPTION (God Did Not Create the Heavens and the Earth):

But if He did, then would there be carbon in organic matter? Would created things have the appearance of age though recently created? – Probably. Certainly, there were rings in trees that God brought into existence. Man did not go through the baby or juvenile stages of growth. He was created mature, etc. Things had the appearance of age. Why not carbon in low content for organic matter? This, in itself, would upset the C-14 time clock.

THIRD ASSUMPTION (The Carbon-14 in the Dead Animal or Plant has neither been Enriched nor Reduced by Chemical Exchange):

But the chance of a particular sample to have been preserved without interaction with its environment is very remote to non-existent.

Physicists use the expression "carbon-14 years" and refuse to say how they relate to the actual chronology. In other words, radiocarbon laboratory workers do not pretend the figures from carbon-14 tests are actual years. They understand the tests represent only relative time periods.

The measurements made in a radiocarbon laboratory do not determine historical ages of dates. The laboratory procedures determine only the amount of radioactive carbon, which a sample contains at present. It is not really possible to state the amount of time that has elapsed from those moments in history when the same sample was taking in C-14 from its environment. To postulate any date or age associated with the sample requires an assumption since it is impossible to know for a certainty the relative amount of C-14 in the environment that supported the life of the organism whose sample is being tested. Interpretation of time elements based on radiocarbon age is not science – it is pure guesswork. Radiocarbon dating is in a crisis because of the third assumption and many more assumptions that could be mentioned. Robert E. Lee writes:

"The troubles of the radiocarbon dating method are undeniably deep and serious ... the underlying *assumptions* have been strongly challenged, and warnings are out that radiocarbon may soon find itself in a crisis situation ... the method depends on a 'fix-it-as-we-go' approach ... It should be no surprise, then, that fully half of the dates are rejected. The wonder is, surely, that the remaining half come[s] to be accepted." [Italics, author]

P. 9

"The radiocarbon method is still not capable of yielding accurate and reliable results. There are gross discrepancies, the chronology is *uneven* and *relative*, and the accepted dates are actually *selected* dates." [Italics, author]

P. 29

[Lee, Robert E., "Radiocarbon Ages In Error," *Anthropological Journal of Canada*, vol. 19, no.3 (1981), pp. 9-29]

QUESTION THIRTY-FIVE:

EVOLUTIONISTS CLAIM RADIOMETRIC DATING PROVES VAST TIME SPANS FOR THE AGE OF THE EARTH AND FOR DINOSAURS, WHICH LIVED IN THE MESOZOIC ERA OF EARTH'S HISTORY. DO CREATIONISTS REGARD RADIOMETRIC DATING TO BE A VALID WAY OF MEASURING THE AGE OF THE EARTH AND DINOSAURS?

ANSWER:

[One can bank on the fact that if a question is asked on Carbon-14, radiometric dating cannot be far behind]

Evolutionists claim that dinosaurs existed on this earth for 225 million years before their extinction. They believe that radiometric dating confirms long ages for the history of the earth with a **current age estimate of about 4.56 billion (4,560,000,000) years.** But, in turn, not every creationist believes as I do, in a young earth. **I suppose you could label me as a "recent-creationist" since *I neither believe in succession nor evolution*. However, there are "ancient-creationists" who reject evolution while at the same time accepting *successive acts of creation over a long period of time*.** Such individuals take the middle road. They neither accept theistic evolution nor do they acknowledge scientific creationism. The same individuals regard my school of thought as "most radical" since I reject radiometric dating as a scientific way of determining the age of the earth. **The bottom line is: One does not have to believe in a young earth to be a creationist and believing in an ancient earth does not automatically make one an evolutionist.**

Radiometric dating does *seem* fool proof: Uniformitarian geologists use many methods for dating rock samples in the earth such as potassium-argon, rubidium-strontium, samarium-neodymium, and lead-lead. **But all these methods of dating are based on the uniformitarian *assumption of unchanging nuclear decay rates in the past*.** However, this ***first assumption* has been proved to be incorrect.** H.C. Dudley has stated that radioactive decay rates, declared to be constant, are "now considered to be a variable ... half lives are NOT constant" (*Industrial Research*, November 15, 1974, P.42).

To state the dating system in a simple manner, evolutionists believe in each case of the above mentioned elements there is a "parent" element that decays into its "daughter" element at a known and slow time rate. These two amounts, found together in the mineral of a rock sample, are measured. The measurement is supposed to indicate the age of the sample in question. *The type of rocks measured for age is igneous.* That is, rock formed by *volcanic action.* Most scientific creationists look at such dating with a critical eye. They are convinced that such methods are unprovable and based on unreasonable assumptions. The following assumptions tell us why radiometric dating only appears to be fool proof.

FIRST ASSUMPTION (The Nuclear Decay Rate Or Half-Life Of The Parent Isotope Has Remained Constant Since The Rock Was Formed. That is, Radioactive Decay Rates Are Constant):

In the above quote, H.C. Dudley, an evolutionary geochronologist, has already informed us as to the fallacious nature of this assumption – "Half lives are not constant." Also, a team of seven scientists (creationists), all members holding an earned doctorate, has completely controverted the assumption, which speaks to the constancy of nuclear decay during the earth's past. **This team is known as RATE (An acronym – *Radioisotopes and the Age of the Earth*). Dr. Don DeYoung, a member of the RATE team of scientists, writes:**

"RATE research has obtained multiple lines of objective physical evidence that nuclear decay rates have been much higher in the past than what we measure today. This evidence can account for why the standard of radioisotope methods often gives ages in the range of millions or billions of years."

Thousands ... Not Billions [Challenging an Icon of Evolution Questioning the Age of the Earth]

P.42

SECOND ASSUMPTION (When the Mineral Rock Is Formed, It Has *No Amount* of Daughter Element Already Present):

The fact is: practically all-igneous rock does have significant amounts of the daughter element already present. These daughter amounts are found in magma that flows from the earth, cools, and becomes crystallized. In the case of modern volcanoes, the same phenomenon is present in the minerals of newly formed lava rocks. Daughter elements are present and rock that is newly formed is calculated to be much older than it really is. This is true for all volcanic rocks since they were all formed in the same way. The calculations, when it comes to radiometric dating methods, are way off since the "apparent" age is immensely greater than the *true age* of the rocks.

P.E Brown and J.A. Miller write:

"Much still remains to be learned of the interpretation of isotopic ages and the realization that *the isotopic age is not necessarily the geologic age of a rock* has led to an over-skeptical attitude by some field geologists." [Emphasis, mine]

"Interpretation of Isotopic Ages in Orogenic Belts," in Kent *et al.* "Time and Place in Orogeny," *Geological Society of London Special*, vol. 3, (1969)

THIRD ASSUMPTION (There Is No Possibility of a Supernatural Creation):

But if there was a creation, then mineral combinations would have parent and daughter elements at their inception. This being so, the rocks would appear to be much older than what they really are. **The old argument is: God has confused mankind because He created rock with the appearance of age. However, if mankind heeded God's revelation in the Bible with reference to the days of creation and the short global time periods, then there would be no need for confusion.**

FOURTH ASSUMPTION (A Rock Has Not Exchanged Atoms with the Surrounding Environment during Its Course of History. In Other Words, the Many Mineral Samples Have Been Closed Systems):

To believe that certain rock can exist for millions of years and form mountains without chemical action exchanges taking place in its environment is to believe the impossible. These allegedly closed systems are really open. An open structure is subject to all kinds of dating problems. For example the individual specimens of rock from the Panamint Mountains in California have dates ranging from 1.09 to 34 billion years. **Thirty-four billion is a ridiculous number that is way beyond the alleged age of the earth.** It is obvious to the evolutionary geochronologists that **the rocks have been enriched,** derived from the adjacent granite and gneiss during Mesozoic metamorphism. G. Faure and J.L. Powell write:

"These results indicate that even total-rock systems may be open during metamorphism and may have their isotopic systems changed, *making it impossible to determine their geologic age." Strontium Isotope Geology* (New York: Springer-Verlag, 1972, P.102) [Emphasis, mine]

What is the conclusion to all of this? The above assumptions cannot be tested, the measurements give inconsistent results, and no radiometric dates are valid. What a tragedy! The public continues to think that radiometric dating is still fool proof. Comninellis writes:

"The public is largely unaware of the unknown assumptions surrounding radiometric dating. By simply changing some of these assumptions, radiometric dates can be brought down to essentially zero. People are also unaware of the fact that many radiometric dating results are wholly inconsistent and are never published.

"The bottom line is that no radiometrically determined date is reliable. Radiometric dating, long considered a secure means of determining age, must be viewed realistically. Though the technique has been perfected for many years, the measurements are based upon unverifiable information, and cannot be trusted."

Creative Defense [Evidence against Evolution]

Comninellis, Nicholas, M.D.

P.108

The *fission track method* should be mentioned because, in a sense, this is also based on radioactivity. High-energy particles shoot off from radioactive material. This leaves damage trails in the rock. Such a phenomenon can actually be observed in transparent rock like mica. It is possible to see the tracks since they have been etched by acid. With this form of dating rock, there are **three problems** ... **1)** such a method, like the ones mentioned above, is also based on the assumption that radioactive decay in the past has been uniform **2)** not all the tracks can be seen **3)** there is a loss of tracks due to heat effects.

Therefore, the fission track method is not reliable. Also, see my final remarks below regarding Uranium-238 – the only significant producer of tracks in terrestrial rocks.

My remarks invite you to note: All the physical processes used by **Uniformitarianists for dating the earth,** none come close to the billions of years deduced from radiometric dating. **This ought to alert anyone to the falsity of this dating method.** For example: let us select one of the techniques – uranium-238 – and trace its feasibility in determining the age of molten rock.

Uranium-238 disintegrates and very slowly passes through a series of intermediate products until it becomes lead-206. Physicists claim that by measuring the proportions of uranium and lead in a rock, they can estimate how long since the rock was molten. This method supposedly dates rocks in millions and billions of years. **Yet in order for this method to be valid, certain assumptions must be true: 1)** The original amount of lead – 206 must be accurately precise **2)** The rate of decay must have remained unchanged **3)** There must have been no gain nor loss of uranium and its decay products from or to the surrounding material.

Creationists respond to this by pointing out, none of the above assumptions can be affirmed since there is no possible way to check them experimentally. Also, without listing them, there are many discrepancies when it comes to samples of rock from various areas. There are volcanoes known to be very young and yet samples indicate the magma to be billions of years old. **This example alone should throw out a red flag to those individuals, who believe in the radiometric dating system.** Thus, the uranium/lead method cannot be depended upon for accurate dating.

One last method of dating rocks and fossils must be discussed – paleomagnetism.

Most people, who have an interest in geology, know about the *relative age* of the earth and fossils. The *concept of superposition* wherein the *oldest* geological bed is on the *bottom* and the *youngest* at the *top* is most understandable. But in the above information, we have been looking at, according to evolutionists, the *specific dating* of beds and fossils.

We have looked at two keys, which supposedly have opened up the doors of specific time periods for various fossils: 1) The technique of radiocarbon dating and 2) Radioactive dating. We have learned the radiocarbon methods are good for dating fossils but not for older ones. For dinosaurs and other very old fossils, radioactive methods allegedly offer the best results. The evolutionists avow that radioactive methods are *very accurate* for dating fossils. However, the meaning of the terms "very accurate" is to be interpreted with caution. That is, there are too many kinks in this dating technique: many inconsistencies, more that a few inaccuracies, the rocks used for dating too often arrive at different dates for the same geological bed that are not even close in comparative studies, and too many anomalies. Scientists admit that there are inconsistencies but these discrepancies in dating are not revealed for public consumption.

With all that we have learned, we must familiarize ourselves with yet another form of comparing ages of geological beds and fossils. Evolutionary scientists claim that the phenomenon (if there is such a phenomenon) of magnetic reversals is the *more accurate method of comparing ages.* **Note that each method of dating is the *most accurate system*! It all depends on what school of thought and theory the scientist happens to be versed in. If the evolutionist has been trained in the theories having to do with the magnetic field of the earth, then *paleomagnetism* is the *most accurate system* for dating the fossil and bed structures.**

Over forty years ago, geophysicists and geologists determined that among many other occurrences, there was another way to figure out the ages of rocks based on paleomagnetism or the behavior of the earth's magnetic fields. It is believed by many evolutionary scientists (but not all) that the earth's core consists of intensely pressurized matter that serves as a *giant dynamo*, which not only provides the mechanical force and energy for moving whole continents around on the earth's surface but also sets up a magnetic field that has a reversal in polarity over great periods of time. The irregular intervals vary between 10,000 years and millions of years.

At this present time, a compass needle aligns itself with magnetic north. Therefore, we are able to tell direction even in the dark and the compass will guard us against getting lost. However, at various intervals through "deep time" the compass (if it could have existed back in time) would point south – 180 degrees opposite from what it should. Christopher McGowan writes:

"These reversals in the Earth's magnetic field are imprinted upon the molten rocks spilling out through the Earth's crust, so that a series of magnetic stripes become locked into the new rocks as they cool down. The stripes can be detected using magnetic devices and, because they vary in their widths, specific stripes can be identified. These have been named and numbered in sequence and provide a means of correlating the ages of rocks in different parts of the world."

Dinosaurs, Spitfires, & Seadragons

P. 295

In other words, the earth's magnetic field is recorded in the rock formations at the earth's surface and geophysicists use this information as a kind of "digital recording." (Jacobs) Evolutionary scientists are supposed to be able to match other rocks of the same age anywhere in the world.

Louis Jacobs makes this candid remark:

"Anywhere rocks exhibit a characteristic pattern of polarity changes, you can be sure they are of the age defined by that magnetic pattern. **Of course, there are any numbers of things that make the real world more complicated than theory**, but in general, that is how Paleomagnetism works for telling geological time. If a specific polarity pattern can be matched up from place to place, the rocks recording the patterns are of the same age. So are the fossils they might contain." [Italics, mine]

Quest for the African Dinosaurs,

P.28

Paleomagnetism is just a theory and not all evolutionary scientists agree with this theory. In fact here are some of the difficulties they are facing in "the real world more complicated than theory."

In the first place, paleomagnetism is **not a technique, which provides an age in number of years.** Before this technique can be applied it *first must depend on the absolute date through the radiometric dating of a volcanic rock.* This being true, the assumptions and discrepancies mentioned above for radiometric dating still apply in this case and makes paleomagnetism as a realistic theory, highly debatable.

In the second place Nicholas Comninellis (a creationist) points out that "research clearly demonstrates that the **earth's magnetic field is rapidly decreasing in strength** ... it is certain that the fall in magnetism is profound; about five percent each century."

He writes:

"If we assume this current rate of decrease has been and will be constant, then two startling conclusions are inevitable. First, within about 1,400 years our magnetic field will disappear entirely. Secondly, if we look backward about 10,000 years, the earth's magnetic field would have been as strong as that of a magnetic star and incapable of supporting life. These conclusions would clearly limit the potential age of the earth to less than 10,000 years."

Creative Defense (Evidence against Evolution)

P.115

Doctor Comninellis quotes evolutionists as the evidence for his rationale: (Anonymous, "Magsat Down, Magnetic Field Declining," *Science News*, vol.117, June, 28, 1980: p.407):

"Preliminary results from the just-downed Magsat – for Magnetic Field Satellite – confirm a previously detected decrease in the intensity of the earth's magnetic field, NASA scientists said last week ....

"Measurements of the main field ... show that the overall intensity of the field is declining at a rate of 26 nanoteslas per year ....

"If the rate of decline were to continue steadily ... the field strength would reach zero in 1,200 years. In that event, according to current theory, the magnetic field would be likely to rebuild with a polarity opposite to that of the present, so that compass needles that now point north would point south.

... Moreover, little is known about what may cause the field, which is created by churning in the earth's molten core, to decline in strength."

[Ibid. Pp. 115-116]

[Special Note: "The magnetic field would be likely to rebuild with a polarity opposite to that of the present, so that compass needles that now point north would point south." This portion of the above quote is supposedly the answer to the creationist argument that the earth's magnetic field is rapidly decreasing in strength and by present day calculations: the earth is thousands of years old and not millions. The evolutionary rationale is, "the present decline is merely a phase in the repeating cycle of reversals." The evolutionists claim that the declining rate of the magnetic field is rapid BUT this decline is merely the results of one cycle before the earth's rebuilding the magnetic field for the next cycle]

However, Henry and John Morris (creationists) are quick to point out:

"One more difficulty should be mentioned in relation to the idea of dipole (two poles of opposite charge an infinitesimal distance apart) reversals. There is a titanic amount of energy associated with the generation of the earth's magnetic field, no matter how it is generated, and that energy will have dissipated when the field decays to zero strength. How then could it ever start up again? The basic energy conservation law would seem to preclude it, unless there is some great (but unknown) source of energy to start up the 'motor' again. And even if there were such a giant 'crank' somewhere in the earth, why would it start up again in the *opposite direction*?"

The Modern Creation Trilogy, Volume Two

P.326

These above creationists point to three other major problems in the theory of magnetic-field reversals ... ...

1) "The main evidence for global magnetic-field reversals (the so-called magnetic 'stripes' on the sea floor on the two sides of the Mid-Atlantic Ridge) has been seriously questioned, if not positively refuted, by the grid of vertical stripes now known to characterize the sea floor magnetization pattern.

2) "Furthermore, these reversals have supposedly been 'dated' to occur at intervals of 500,000 to 700,000 years. But if the present decay cycle – which is scheduled to reach zero in the next 1,000 to 2,000 years – has been going on for 500,000 years, the earth long since *would have been vaporized* under the intense heat generated by the decaying electric currents, or dynamo motions, or whatever is producing the magnetic field in the earth's deep interior.

3) "It is true that there is much evidence of former magnetic reversals now preserved in various basaltic rocks and other igneous formations at a number of places around the earth, including some that suggest much shorter periods of reversal (e.g., reversed polarity within a single lava-flow rock) but there is no compelling evidence that any of these represent *global* reversals of the magnetic field, rather than ephemeral local phenomena."

Henry and John Morris contend, "There are, in fact, still many reputable geophysicists and geologists (not just creationists) who question the whole concept."

"See, for example, the symposium *New Concepts in Global Tectonics*, eds. S. Chatterjee and N. Holton (Lubbock, TX: Texas Tech University Press, 1992). This compilation contains 23 papers by geophysicists and other scientists who reject the plate tectonics paradigm, and propose various other theories to explain the same phenomena" (This is a footnote in "The Modern Creation Trilogy Science & Creation," volume two, P.325).

There are reputable scientists, who do not believe this earth to have at its core a great dynamo full of tremendous energy that is capable of moving whole continents around on the earth's surface or, among many other so-called phenomena, magnetic reversals.

Creationists can only do likewise in their rejection of the paleomagnetism system of dating and the theory of magnetic reversals. **Creationists would agree with Louis Jacobs, "the real world [is] more complicated than theory." The reversals in earth's magnetic field are not part of the real world of empirical science and the whole system of magnetic dating lacks sufficient evidence and, therefore, making the subject of earth's supposedly liquid iron core to somehow generate a magnetic field, as highly speculative.**

FORMAT II (DINOSAUR EXTINCTION)

THE ULTIMATE QUESTIONS POSED BY ALL CREATIONISTS AND EVOLUTIONISTS – *HOW* **DID THE DINOSAURS DIE? AND** *WHY* **DID THEY DIE?**

QUESTION THIRTY-SIX:

CREATIONISTS CLAIM THAT THE DINOSAURS PERISHED IN THE NOACHIAN FLOOD. BUT SCIENTISTS HAVE EVIDENCE THAT DINOSAURS BECAME EXTINCT THROUGH OTHER CAUSES. WHAT MAKES THE CREATIONISTS THINK THEY ARE CORRECT IN THEIR ASSERTIONS AND SCIENTISTS ARE WRONG IN THEIR AFFIRMATIONS?

ANSWER:

[Obviously, the question of dinosaur extinction will be posited in every series of meetings. The following thoughts are an extended version of the shortened answers given in public. QUESTION THIRTY-SIX is both an anticipated question and book style written for my readers]

On the one hand, creationists who believe in the Flood are much aware that many dinosaurs did die from the time of the fall until the moment of the Great Flood. Dinosaurs expired through natural death, disease, natural disasters, accidents, prey for predators, etc. On the other hand, not all creationists believe that the dinosaur descendants perished in the Noachian Flood. In fact, there are three viewpoints:

1) No dinosaur descendants were taken into the Ark. All of them were destroyed in the Flood.

2) All kinds of dinosaurs were taken into the Ark, including herbivorous sauropods and carnivorous types of theropods.

3) All kinds of land animals but not every kind of dinosaur was taken into the Ark. The carnivorous species and the huge species of dinosaurs were not taken in because of their threat to humankind.

Most creationists, who believe certain or all dinosaur kinds were taken into the ark, also conclude that these dinosaurs died out within the next 700 years after disembarking on Mt. Ararat. Their final demise was eventually due to cold climate and food shortage. Because of volcanic activity during and following the time of the Flood, much ash was in the air. The global temperatures were lowered and the dinosaurs were unable to cope with the cold weather conditions brought on by the Ice Age. Therefore, many dinosaurs were unable to find food and eventually starved to death. However, a massive amount of dinosaurs did perish in the flood. This is how most recent-creationists explain the large number of dinosaur fossils found throughout most regions of the earth. Thus, it is virtually true – the Flood is the big issue for explaining dinosaur extinction by the creationist.

The formulator of our original question is correct in stating that scientists affirm the extinction of dinosaurs "through other causes." **In fact, 80 to a 100 theories are on the list of possible causes for dinosaur extinction. The evidence for these causes is questionable and evolutionists debate, at great length, with one another.**

Each scientist has his own pet theory, which, at times, is passionately defended. This fact explains *the abundance of theories* since there is *a wealth of scientists.*

Evolutionists claim that dinosaurs died out about 65 million years ago. At the end of the Cretaceous Period, according to evolutionists, there was a sudden disappearance of all dinosaurs. This is difficult to explain since dinosaur groups showed no indicators that would even hint at their "mysterious" demise.

Dr. David Norman, an evolutionist, writes:

"One of the eternal questions asked of any paleontologist is 'why did the dinosaurs become extinct?' It is a question that has haunted us all ever since it was first noted that dinosaurs did not appear to leave descendants in the Cenozoic Era, following the Cretaceous Period."

The Prehistoric World of the Dinosaur

P.146

Norman is not being sensational when he uses the word "haunted." The entire issue of dinosaur extinction actually does pester and harass scientists. **Dinosaurs were strong, robust, healthy, sturdy, muscular, and all groups seemed to be perfected for their various ecological environments.** *Why* **should all of them suddenly vanish?**

In a close study of dinosaur characteristics, there are no evidences, which would remotely suggest inherent weaknesses eventually leading to their sudden death. Whenever scientists attempt to give reasons for dinosaur extinction, **they use the word "mystery." This term is often used to describe complete helplessness when it comes to manufacturing reasons for the Great Extinction or the Great Dying.**

A mystery is something unexplainable and highly complex – the very reason explanations remain unsatisfactory and the theoretical nature of them prove to be unacceptable and refuted with not much trouble. What makes it difficult to dispense altogether with such theories? In some cases, coupled with pure theory, there is an inherent logical basis for the scientist's premise. However, such a basis is not always considered to be true in every instance. As we shall soon observe, some theories are absurd. In fact, a number of the theories are taken as a gag but a few are given consideration due to the serious attempt to establish them on a scientific basis.

Since I am dealing with the ***ultimate question,*** there will be an extensive rundown of the various viewpoints circulated throughout the camp of evolutionists. I have made no attempt at arranging these theories into a logical order. You may find some of them interesting as well as challenging.

VIEWS OF EVOLUTIONISTS CONCERNING DINOSAUR EXTINCTION
AND THE REASONS FOR REJECTION

1) Dinosaurs could not cope with new plants appearing in the Middle Cretaceous since they not only contained protective chemicals and might have poisoned the dinosaurs but the new plants were hard to digest and gave the dinosaurs constipation.

This theory is rejected by evolutionary scientists due to their acceptance of long ages for the geological time divisions. They reason that the dinosaurs died out at the *end of the Cretaceous*, not in the middle. Therefore, dinosaurs had eaten these plants and flowers for over 40 million years. Why did such a diet not bother them for so many years and then suddenly destroy them in a short time span?

2) Small mammals ate all the dinosaur eggs and this brought about dinosaur extinction.

But is this really a good explanation for the eventual annihilation of dinosaurs? This theory is unlikely for at least six reasons:

* True, there is evidence for dinosaurs laying eggs but it is not known that all dinosaurs laid eggs. If there were live births, then these species probably would have survived.

* In the world today, there are animal species that eat eggs on a daily basis. Yet, there is no evidence that such a diet is causing extinction of any known animals.

* Nature seems to maintain a balance of predator and prey. It is unlikely a species would be eaten out of existence.

* Sometimes, mammals probably did eat dinosaur eggs. However, it would have taken a tremendous number of mammals to devour all the dinosaur eggs. Therefore, this is an unlikely explanation for a sudden major extinction. The *mammal-dinosaur egg ratio* rules out such a theory.

* Many other types of animals beside dinosaurs died out at the end of the Cretaceous. Therefore, egg-eating mammals could hardly be responsible for *mass extinction.*

* Evolutionists believe mammals were probably eating dinosaur eggs for millions of years. Why would such a diet suddenly be responsible for dinosaur extinction?

3) The dinosaurs died out because they evolved too much.

This is one of the older theories and not acceptable. To say dinosaurs became too big and too specialized and they could not adjust to a fluctuating world is simply not true. Dinosaurs were quite intelligent and were well able to adjust to their surroundings. They lived for many years and no one theory is adequate to explain what actually happened to bring about the end of dinosaurs.

4) There is the "world-weariness" theory. That is, the dinosaurs lived long enough and it was time for them to go.

Hardly does this theory seem feasible since there were so *many new types* at the end of the so-called Cretaceous Period.

5) The fatal body disorders. Dinosaurs, because of their large body size, died from slipped discs. Also, diminishing brain size resulted in death through stupidity.

This theory also comes up short. The late dinosaurs had large brains and few dinosaurs in the fossil record show evidence of spine damage.

6) Because of crowding, female dinosaurs came under great stress, which affected the thickness of their eggs. The thinning of the eggshells was subject to damage, which caused which caused dinosaurs to die out.

Actually, the discovery of large nesting areas refuted this theory. Therefore crowding did not induce thin shells because of stress, pressure, or anxiety. Prior to the discovery of the large nesting sights, giving proof that overcrowding did not cause stress, elaborate development of the thin eggshell theory persisted. It was claimed the stress in dinosaurs caused an imbalance of the delicate hormonal system. This, in turn, led to a decrease in clutch size and shell thickness. Thin shells can crack and such shells lack the calcium that is necessary for embryos to absorb for the building of their skeletal system. The paleontologists, who advocated this theory, said the weak-shelled eggs fixed the fate of dinosaur offspring. [Certainly, such a sophisticated theory gives the appearance of logic but logic does not always lead to the truth of a matter. From the above, one can readily deduce a theory may appear to be strong on the surface and still lack scientific substantiation]

7) Robert Bakker, as I might have supposed, has a fairly good theory for explaining dinosaur extinction. He claims that at the end of the Cretaceous, there was an intercontinental exchange of animal species. That is, continents moved together and land bridges were formed. This enabled dinosaurs to travel into new areas after leaving their old habitats. Dinosaurs, in mixing their faunas, were subjected to many diseases. They came into contact with parasites and disease organisms against which they had no means of resistance. Dinosaur systems had no build-up immunities for protection against new organisms and died as a result. This theory could easily be called "death by faunal mixing."

Again, this is good logic but no actual proof for this position. [However, in the reading of many dinosaur books, I am not aware of an opposing argument. But difficulties for me are: how far away were these continents before they moved together and whether or not these particular continents with their animals, contained parasites peculiar to their particular region. I consider parasites to be among the most dangerous creatures to inhabit the earth. Bakker's theory is a gruesome proposition. I would have to know how parasites come to inhabit a certain area and how they are transmitted from one organism to another. At this point in time, I simply do not have the knowledge that would allow making a fair and honest comment concerning faunal mixing and disease. At the present moment I am reading Carl Zimmer's book, "Parasite Rex" in hoping to learn something about these creatures from this science journalist who is an evolutionist. I know there are creationists who specialize in parasitological studies but so far I am acquainted with only a smattering of information]

8) Dinosaurs were killed by some great catastrophe such as a deadly global dust cloud that had arisen from vast volcanic eruptions such as those that built India's great Deccan Plateau.

There are quite a few theories like this one geared for the rapid disappearance of dinosaurs. On the other hand, many evolutionists believe there was a gradual dinosaur decline. Dinosaurs and other animal species gradually sputtered out due to geological phenomena such as shifting continents, rising mountains, and shrinking seas of which helped new variations of animals to overcome the old.

At this point, I would like to return to part of the original question – "What makes the creationists think they are correct in their assertion and scientists are wrong in their affirmations?" Creationists can reasonably conclude that the affirmations of evolutionary scientists are, indeed, wrong since there are so many conflicting notions. Under this 8th reason that evolutionists give for dinosaur extinction, there are two conflicting views of extinction – rapid and gradual. **When scientists line up on one side or the other, which side should be considered acceptable science? Both sides cannot be right at the same time.** Also, there is no rational reason for creationists to view this hodgepodge of questionable information as anything else but wrong and inaccurate and to think evolutionists are incorrect in their reasons advanced for the demise of the dinosaur kingdoms.

The honest attempt that men make in coming to correct conclusions is not reason enough for transforming theories into acceptable facts. Creationists find 80 to 100 conflicting viewpoints, unacceptable for explaining the death of the dinosaur dynasty. Most creationists, with assuredness, turn to the Flood theory since the *Flood model* is filled with the empirical *facts of nature.*

A final block of reasons for dinosaur extinction will now be presented. We have taken a quick look at some of the various theories, which included a food-related cause, mental-physical reasons, a disease-related explanation, an atmospheric cause, etc. Let us consider the final examples of dinosaur termination – extraterrestrial impact. **The impact theories are fast gaining adherents since they have been popularized publicly:**

* A "bomb" from space was responsible for the eradication of dinosaurs. That is, an asteroid punched through a weak spot in the earth's crust. In turn, this phenomenon activated an enormous volcanic eruption. The volcanic dust clouds lowered the earth's temperature and annihilated the dinosaurs.

* Another version has an immense meteorite striking the earth and throwing out a huge dust cloud that blocked the rays of the sun. Plants, deprived of the sunlight, died out. Vegetarian-type dinosaurs, cut off from the food chain, died. Many other dinosaurs died in chilling lands, which suffered a reduction in temperature because of the great dust cloud.

Many scientists believe that proof for the asteroid strike is evidenced in large amounts of metal iridium in clay bands. This event allegedly took place 65 million years ago at the exact time of dinosaur extinction. However, the case for an asteroid strike is not indisputable nor without its weakness.

Iridium deposits are not irrefutable evidence for supporting the theory of extraterrestrial impact. The following rationale discounts the iridium level theory:

*Walter Alvarez first noted iridium levels. He reasoned that a large meteor, after smashing into the earth, would send up vast clouds of iridium-rich dust. The dust settled back onto the earth's surface and melted. Alvarez concluded this event killed the dinosaurs. Many consider this theory, to be rather weak because of its selectivity. An extraterrestrial event such as this should have destroyed most animals and yet the meteor seemed to pick out only certain species in the animal kingdom. Marine reptiles disappeared along with the dinosaurs. Ammonites also became extinct. Flying reptiles – the pterosaurs – suffered a similar fate. Yet other animals escaped extinction – turtles, birds, frogs, crocodiles, and mammals. Thus, many species died off and many others survived the alleged catastrophe. Again, such selectivity is highly unlikely.

*Since asteroids do contain the iridium element; evolutionary geologists (many of them) accept the iridium levels to be the conclusive argument for the asteroid collision that destroyed the dinosaurs. But are iridium deposits the result of a single asteroid explosion? The earth's geology strongly indicates another possible explanation for iridium levels: the earth's core contains iridium and at times, this iridium is brought up and re-deposited by volcanic eruption. Therefore, an asteroid strike is not the only explanation for iridium levels.

*Iridium is buried in tons of hardened mud and sands called sediments. While many evolutionists point to iridium as the basis for the asteroid-impact theory, creationists point to the sediments containing iridium as basis for a differing argument. That is, the thousands of feet of sedimentary sandstone, shale, and limestone strongly imply that *other Great Catastrophe such as the Noachian Flood.*

*The asteroid-impact theory calls for a six-mile-wide asteroid. Such an asteroid would have caused a tremendous crater hole. Scientists have not discovered such evidence although there are some who believe that certain geophysical maps of 1991, give supporting evidence for a Yucatan Cretaceous/Tertiary boundary crater. Scientists claim to detect half a crater rim (the rest being under water) that is estimated to be 120 miles wide. Figuring the crater diameter and the diameter of the asteroid itself (six miles), geologists have calculated the impact explosion. They claim that such a strike would be 10,000 times more powerful than an explosion comparable to all this earth's atomic weapons set off together. The crater has been named "Chicxulub" for its hub town. In the Mayan language, Chicxulub means, "tail of the devil." There are many scientists who see this identification as a "smoking gun." That is, there is still much to be proved in identifying this region as a true crater-remnant and the one, which points to the past asteroid, killer of dinosaurs. James Lawrence Powell has written, *Night Comes to the Cretaceous*. He identifies Chicxulub as the killer asteroid. His book is a credible expose. He is an evolutionist whose arguments are well thought out. Creationists should read this book to understand that opposing positions can be strong and logical. Notwithstanding, there are many other evolutionists who reject his position. They still believe impact theories fail to explain why dinosaurs would die out but many other forms of life would continue to survive. Such survivors included insects, birds, mammals, flowering and freshwater plants, and a variety of sea life species.

*Another point, which befuddles the asteroid-impact theory, is the demise of certain creatures from the Mesozoic group called *ammonites*. For many scientists, the death of the ammonites coinciding with dinosaur extinction is rather difficult to explain.

Ammonites, they say, became extinct at the end of the Cretaceous but could an asteroid-impact induce changes in the atmosphere leading to the death of the ammonites? Many believe the answer to be in the negative and, therefore, weakening the impact theory. The ammonites were cephalopods somewhat like the living pearly nautilus, though frequently much larger. These forms of life were very resilient and, since they were easily able to feed and scavenge at various levels in the ocean, it is difficult to believe they would have become extinct during and after an asteroid-impact with earth.

I have covered some of the evolutionary viewpoints regarding the demise of the dinosaurian kingdoms. **Many weaknesses have been pointed out in these theories but the criticisms have arisen from the ranks of evolutionists – not creationists.** Returning to the original question proposed by an evolutionist and regarding dinosaur extinction; it is not a matter of the creationists thinking the affirmations of certain scientists are wrong; *their own colleagues think they are wrong.* Evolutionists have already made the charges but creationists will second them.

Evidences must be presented why most creationists direct attention to the biblical Flood as the reason for dinosaur extinction. The truth of their assertion: the Flood was the cause of the Great Dying of the dinosaurs, recorded in the fossil record and evidenced in the geological column, will now be affirmed by examples from geology and paleontology.

VIEWS OF CREATIONISTS CONCERNING DINOSAUR EXTINCTION AND THE REASONS FOR ACCEPTANCE

Geology – Sedimentary Rock

In order to establish the demise of dinosaurs through Universal Flood action, it is necessary first of all to be aware of geological evidences for such a Flood. One of the first things a student of geology is taught: sedimentary rocks cover about 75 percent of the earth's land surface. Actually, the amount of sediment is even higher since some of the metamorphic rocks were sedimentary rock types prior to metamorphism.

Clyde L. Webster, Jr. writes:

"The most unique feature of these stratified sediments is not their thickness but their similarities and their wide range of distribution. Many strata can be traced over thousands of square miles and from continent to continent. Some extend over much of the world!

"Strata identical to the English 'White cliffs of Dover' can be found in France, Germany, Scandinavia, Poland, Bulgaria, and Russia. Similar chalk deposits of the same geologic age and characteristics can also be found in Texas, Arkansas, Mississippi and Alabama in North America. And, last but not least, similar chalk deposits can be found also in Western Australia! All of these deposits are resting on the same type of glauconitic sandstone!"

A Scientist's Perspective on Creation and the Flood

Pp.15-16

Sedimentary rock reveals geological features that are neither explainable by the doctrine of uniformity nor in agreement with the natural course of events. Webster, in the above statements, presents strong evidence for a Universal Flood. Such conformation not only contradicts the basic assumption of uniformity, which is the basis of the evolutionist's geology, but supports the creationist who believes in the Flood as the fabric of geology.

One more statement on sedimentary rock by Harold W. Clark:

"If we travel over the Colorado Plateau, which covers much of Utah and bordering states, we would find extensive cross-bedded shales and sandstones, with lenticular beds, laid down on the truncated surfaces below. Some of these beds are comparatively thin, but spread out quite regularly over a vast area of 100,000 square miles or more. How such deposits could have taken place without violent and widespread waves of water is impossible to imagine."

Fossils, Flood, and Fire

P.32

Such deposits are indicative of a Great Catastrophic event (the biblical Flood) and could have supplied the force of water action necessary to expunge dinosaurs from the face of the earth.

Geology – Coal Beds

Evolutionists, leaning on the crutch of uniformity, advance the notion that coal beds have been produced in bogs over a period of 50,000,000 years or more. A bog is waterlogged ground that consists primarily of mosses. It contains acidic, decaying vegetation. This can turn to peat and, under pressure, can achieve relatively high carbon content and turns to coal.

Uniformitarianists teach such a process takes millions of years and that coal seams form from the vegetation that grows in place. The above description is the peat-bog theory simplified. However, there is no amount of vegetation on the earth, and growing in one place, that could account for the thickness of some coal seams. The peat-bog theory is not an adequate explanation for coal beds. How then, did the beds form? Obviously, in order to procure enough vegetation for coal formations, the plant growth had to be washed in from other areas. This could have been accomplished by a Universal Flood, providing the currents necessary to transport large amounts of vegetation into earth's continental depressions as well as into other landmass areas.

Webster writes:

"The origin of such vast coal beds has been an area of major study for many geologists. Any uniformitarian model developed by geologists cannot accommodate the immense size or depth of the majority of the coal beds. However, the concept of a global flood that eroded out the forests and plant cover of the pre-flood world, collected it in great floating mats of debris, and then deposited it in sinking basins seems to be a reasonable model which can account for the great extent and thickness of the coal beds."

A Scientist's Perspective on Creation and the Flood

Clyde L. Webster, Jr.

P.16

Any water action that is extensive enough to form deposits of large amounts of vegetation for the formation of coal is not the result of uniformity or any natural phenomenon. Coal is another memorial of the Flood and of a catastrophic-geology. Any flood that is capable of performing this action is far more capable of annihilating dinosaurs. The above examples will suffice for demonstrating the truth of the biblical Flood. **Creationists are certain that studies in geology lean favorably towards evidence for the biblical Flood and far away from the pseudo-philosophy of uniformity. Thus, creationists do believe their affirmation concerning a Global Flood is correct. They also believe the main body of dinosaurs met their demise in this same Flood. The truth of this affirmation is also backed by paleontology.**

Paleontology – Dinosaur Graveyards

Since the geological evidence gives ample support to the Great Flood and the feasibility of dinosaur extermination, creationists affirm paleontology evidence can do no less. It should not be a difficult task to establish dinosaur graveyards to be additional testimony in establishing the demise of dinosaurs through Universal Flood action.

Many dinosaur graveyards studied by paleontologists, attest to quick burial by catastrophic flood action. A number of graveyards will serve as examples to the Great Dying of Dinosaurs caused by the Flood.

NORTH AMERICA:

* **Cleveland – Lloyd quarry** in central Utah is packed with predatory dinosaurs. Paleontologists have concluded this was an obvious predator kill site. Four-dozen meat eating *Allosaurus Atrox* was among the fossils. There are 18,000 bones, which have been removed from this Utah quarry, and how they came to rest in this particular area is quite mystifying to dinosaurologists. They reason that dinosaurs were attracted to the lush vegetation, became trapped in the mud, and were easy prey for predators. But a major problem is evident when one is confronted with the fact: *herbivorous dinosaurs are missing* from the quarry.

Three quarters of the bones recovered are Allosaurus – a fierce meat eater. The scenario that would have this area in Utah, designated as a kill site is, to say the least, very shaky since no herbivores have been discovered. Where are the vegetarian eating dinosaurs? The bones in the quarry are disarticulated and mixed together. This speaks of mass destruction. There are other paleontologists, who believe the quarry is the result of dinosaurs having been killed by flooding. This observation better fits the creationists' viewpoint of a Universal Flood.

* **Dinosaur National Monument,** in northeast Utah is unique. It has a broad representation of many different types of dinosaurs. The entangled remains are within coarse conglomerate. The remains include Allosaurus, Stegosaurus, Barosaurus, Diplodocus, and Apatosaurus. A building covers the 200-foot face of a rock wall in which the dinosaur bones are embedded. Rock has been removed from the bones so that they stand in relief. Geologists and paleontologists assess there were periodic catastrophes attributed to fast moving water. Water is the key fact in dinosaur burial at the Dinosaur National Monument.

Geologists can determine the water was fast moving simply by examining the size of the rounded to subangular fragments in the matrix. If the fragments in the sediments are large, then they could have transported into place only by fast moving and powerful currents of water. The geologists believe there were periodic floods. This is deduced by observing various levels of sediment. However, creationists conclude the levels could have been formed within the same short time span as one Great Flood washed in the sediments from different areas. The bones of the dinosaurs are crushed, broken, and disarticulated, attesting to the fact of a violent burial. The almost vertical wall in to which dinosaurs are packed was due to the break-up and movements of the earth during the Great Flood.

* **Ghost Ranch quarry** is located in New Mexico and was discovered in 1947. The quarry contains several thousand *Coelophysis* skeletons. "How the quarry came to be is not fully understood" (Gregory S. Paul). "Even more puzzling is the cause of their death … the exact cause remains a mystery" (Sylvia and Stephen Czerkas).

Evolutionists are not prepared to venture a guess as to what natural catastrophe caused the demise of the Coelophysids. Although fire, floods, disease, or accidental poisoning have been mentioned.

The creationist is not out of order, when the Great Flood is suggested as being the true cause of death. Certainly, such a large body of species would have necessitated quick burial for the preservation of their remains. This would call for flooding action, such as could only be provided by the biblical Flood. As to why there was an extremely large concentration of these animals that was excessive for the numbers expected in a single pack or herd, the following idea is proposed. The possibility of more than one herd uniting in their quick retreat from the phenomena of the Great Flood is not an inconceivable scenario. [For more detail on the Ghost Ranch quarry, the reader is referred to Pittack's book, *The Archaeopteryx Controversy*, Chapter 12 and (2) Dinosaur Graveyards]

* There are mass graveyards of Maiasaura (Duckbill dinosaurs) in **western Montana.** These hadrosaurs (a species of duckbill) number about 10,000 in the extensive bone bed – according to estimates. Along with volcanic action, dinosaurologists believe another event followed this – torrential amounts of water inundated the area and currents of flooding waters transported the bones over broad plains. For creationists, this is a perfect picture of biblical Flood action. Creationists, in the majority, have always linked volcanic action and flooding for two of the many forces, which compromised the Great Flood event. Geologists and paleontologists have deduced possible explanations for the Maiasaura deposits. Some felt that a mudslide was solely responsible and others leaned towards mud plus late flood action.

The mudslide theory posited problems. Scientists had no explanation for the source of the catastrophic mudflow. Where did all this mud come from? Also, the bones are in terrible condition – a fact not easy to explain by mudflow burial. Another problem – there are hardly any small bones such as toes and fingers. Mud would preserve them, along with other bones, by keeping them from flowing far off from anatomical parts. Again, there are hardly any adjacent skulls. This does not seem reasonable in light of the mudflow theory. Thus, other scientists saw the need for adding water action in their summary of quarry events. This would, at least, explain how small body parts could be missing. They were, because of their lightweight, washed away. The skulls, easily becoming disengaged from the main body, could have been washed away in strong water currents.

However, where did the water come from since the bones are not positioned in a river or streambed? Some theorize that a river broke its boundaries and provided the necessary water currents. This hardly seems to be the answer since the volume of lake water for producing such force, could not be catastrophic as they claim. Unless, of course, the lake was at a much higher elevation, contained the right amount of cubic miles of water, and had one of its sides breached. Once again, the creationist should not be denied the setting forth of the Flood theory. It is just as logical that the biblical Flood transported the mud from far-off areas, provided the necessary currents for carrying off body parts, and caused the bad conditions of bones, which were tumbled and tossed by flood energy.

* **Landslide Butte** is a coined name given by Jack Horner to a place in Montana just this side of the Canadian border. He said, "Landslide Butte was a shock."

Don Lessem writes about Landslide Butte:

"Here was a site so rich in fossils that Horner has estimated 53 million bone pieces can be found in the space of a few square miles. In this spot duckbills nested and died by the tens of thousands, killed suddenly by a local catastrophe, likely a drought."

P.265

Must millions of dinosaur bones and duckbills, dying by the tens of thousands, be the result of a local catastrophe? No matter how extensive the graveyard sites, evolutionists, without fail, always manage to stay clear of a Universal Catastrophe and boil it down to a local calamity. How many thousands of these local catastrophes must there be to finally add up to the overall picture of a Universal Flood? Jack Horner was shocked to witness such an assemblage of dinosaur bones. But why should he be shocked? – The entire earth on which he stands is a vast assemblage of fossilized animals – a graveyard, if you please. The devastation that he witnessed is only a part of the wholesale destruction. Most of the fossils, which we know of, died in sedimentary rock and were quickly buried. "Fossils from every part of the world constitute convincing evidence for the biblical Flood" (Rehwinkel).

SOUTH AMERICA: South America has rich bone beds of dinosaurs. There are over three-dozen named genera from four nations. This continent is mentioned briefly only to give the idea that it is another continent that contains dinosaur graveyards. All continents have dinosaur remains, which are a strong indication that the Flood was universal in scope.

AFRICA: Africa has famous bone yards of dinosaurs in Niger and Tanzania. Mud preserved the skeletons of these dinosaurs drowned by ancient flooding. From 1909 to 1912, German expeditions paid 500 Africans to dig pits from which they uncovered many thousands of bones. Collectors shipped to Germany 1000 boxes of fossils totaling 250 tons. Creationists rightly assume this is further evidence of a biblical Flood. What other force could have preserved so many dinosaurs in one cataclysmic event?

ASIA:

1) **Mongolia** – There are rich bone-beds in the deserts of Mongolia. The Nemegt Basin alone holds a huge graveyard, which contains thousand of dinosaur bones, including duckbills, sauropods, theropods, and other species all drowned by flooding.

2) In **China**, flooding of inland basins drowned countless dinosaurs. The Sichuan Basin alone has yielded hundreds of dinosaurs. This area is recognized as the place of "amazing" bone beds.

3) The **quarry of Dashaupu** is located in the Zigong province of China. There is a large assortment of dinosaurs, many of them tumbled and torn. There were Shunosaurus dinosaurs (with their armor-spiked tail clubs), carnivorous saurischian, and ornithischian dinosaurs. Along with the dinosaurs, there are winged pterosaurs and various fish. Raging water, mud, stone, and debris entombed them. Scientists attributed all this to a flash flood (in fact, most fossilized forms are allegedly the result of flash floods). However, along with these fossilized animals, there are also huge fallen trees, tens of meters in length, and all wonderfully preserved. Such a scenario causes one to wonder how a flash flood could topple over such large trees and then provide the volume of sediments necessary to cover and preserve them.

EUROPE: A final dinosaur burial is open for consideration. In 1878, in the village of Bernissart in Belgium, coal miners discovered bones of the dinosaur *Iguanodon* (a large plant-eating dinosaur that grew up to 30 feet long and weighed close to 5 tons). The Royal Museum of Natural History (Belgium) uncovered 39 skeletons. There are a variety of theories as to how these creatures died and were entombed. How does one account for the remarkable accumulation of skeletons in one area of interment? [For the details of these theories and the possible concluding answer, the reader is referred to Pittack's book, *The Archaeopteryx Controversy,* Chapter 12 and (2) Dinosaur Graveyards]

A number of things are evident in this burial: In order for fossilization to take place, there had to be immediate burial. The clay and sandstone levels, in which the Iguanodons were entombed, were water deposited. In fact, all sedimentary rock is formed by solid fragmental material, transported mainly by water, and deposited in layers. There is at least one theory that *associates flooding with burial of the Iguanodons.*

Creationists would suggest the Iguanodons were swept in to the ravine, buried by a vast aqueous catastrophe, and were entombed. While evolutionists compete one with another for the plausibility of their particular theory, creationists have as much right to present the logic and credibility of their understanding of the Belgium dinosaurs' burial.

CONCLUSION ON

DINOSAUR EXTINCTION

Winding up my remarks to the question posed many pages ago, much evidence has been presented to demonstrate the ideas associated with dinosaur extinction are only of a theoretical nature. Evolutionists contradict one another and yes, they are wrong but simply by the act of criticism leveled by their own colleagues with the creationists seconding the motion. Most of the bowdlerization leveled at the various theories of dinosaur extinction has come straight from the ranks of evolutionists. They are the ones responsible for the refutation of their own theories regarding the eradication of dinosaurs. **One by one, theories have been undermined and damaged *by their own words*. With 80 to 100 extinction theories of a speculative element, who should be declared the arbiter of truth? On the other hand creationists, *who also have their theories*, feel that their *affirmations are true* since the facts of nature fit the Flood Model much better than they fit the Uniformity Model. The Flood Model is supported by the *empirical facts* within the *geological and paleotological systems.***

Dinosaurs were obliterated from off the face of the globe. Their kind is unknown except for what has been preserved in the fossil record. [The idea that birds are dinosaurs and that dinosaurs are not truly extinct, is another issue. But it is a myth that all dinosaurologists believe in the dinosaur-bird theory. Please refer to my book, *The Archaeopteryx Controversy*. This book gets into the bird-dinosaur connection in intense detail]

Evolutionists consider dinosaur extinction to be a mystery. They still find it difficult to explain why dinosaurs perished simultaneously over all the earth and how they were massed together in large cemeteries. Creationists do not find dinosaur extinction to be a mystery. They believe the answers and solution are contained within the biblical account of the Flood Catastrophe and it is reasonable to conclude water is the only agent that could bring about the necessary conditions for dinosaur destruction and their burial on so wide a scale. **The geological formations, upon and within the earth, point to catastrophic events induced by aqueous energy of supernatural origin. The facts of geology and paleontology negate the doctrine of uniformitarianism, which states that forces observable can only explain past geologic events today.**

In closing FORMAT II, I will contrast two writings. The first comes from the thoughts of a respected writer on dinosaurs and a remarkable artist of the same – **Gregory S. Paul**. The second comes from the mind of **King David,** who lived over three thousand years ago.

Dinosaurologist Paul writes:

"In sum, we do not know what killed off the theropods, their prey, and the primitive birds – while allowing advanced birds to pass through … those who claim the question has been resolved are jumping the gun. What is needed is far more data from late Cretaceous and earliest Tertiary deposits around the world. Until then, we will remain in the dark."

Predatory Dinosaurs of the World

Pp.81-82

King David writes:

"How sweet are thy words unto my taste! Yea, sweeter than honey to my mouth! Through thy precepts I get understanding: therefore I hate every false way. **Thy word is a lamp unto my feet, and a light unto my path.**"

Psalm 119: 103-105 KJV

By an evolutionist's own words, there is an admission that dinosaur extinction is a subject for which no answers have been found. **Paleontologists *remain in the dark with no immediate light* to resolve their enigma.**

On the other hand, the creationist King David has declared that *God has given light through His word – the Bible.*

Creationists accept the light, which God has revealed throughout the Scriptures and especially, in the book of Genesis. The book of Genesis is one of the most important books ever written and it is the only clear and inspired scientific document ever written which opens up the secrets of geology and paleontology. **If Genesis were accepted by the "scientific world" there would be great light to illuminate those areas enshrouded by mystery and darkness – particularly the extinction of most animal life including the dinosaurs.**

Moses writes:

"The secret things belong unto the LORD our God: but those *things that are revealed* belong unto us and to our children forever."

Deuteronomy 29:29 KJV

Finally Paul writes:

"For whatsoever *things* were written aforetime *were written for our learning,* that we through patience and comfort of the scriptures might have hope."

Romans 15:4 KJV

SOURCES

QUESTION ONE

Desmond, Adrian J., *The Hot Blooded Dinosaurs A Revolution In* Paleontology, The Dial Press/James Wade, New York, 1976, first published in Great Britain by Blond & Briggs Ltd., copyright © 1975 by Adrian J. Desmond, Pp. 14, 17.

Han, Ken; Sarfati, Jonathan; Wieland, Carl; edited by Ballen, *Don, The Revised & Expanded Answers Book*, Master Book, thirtieth printing: April 2004. Copyright © 1990 by Creation Science Foundation, P.241.

Genesis 1:24-27; 6:19

QUESTION TWO

Jacobs, Louis, *Quest for the African Dinosaurs*, Villard Books, New York, 1993, Copyright © 1993 by Louis L. Jacobs, P.245.

QUESTION THREE

The Seventh-day Adventist Bible Commentary in Seven Volumes, Volume 1, Genesis to Deuteronomy, Review and Herald Publishing Association, Washington; D.C., Copyright, 1954, by the Review and Herald Publishing Association.

Psihoyos, Louie with Knoebber, John, *Hunting Dinosaurs*, Random House, Inc., New York, Copyright © 1994 by Louie Psihoyos, P.220.

Svarney, Thomas E. and Svarney-Barnes, Patricia, *The Handy Dinosaur Book*, Visible Ink Press, Farmington Hills, MI, copyright © 2000 by Visible Ink Press ®, P.269.

QUESTION FOUR

White, E.G., *Patriarchs and Prophets*, Pacific Press Publishing Association, Mountain View, California, Copyright 1890, 1913, by Mrs. E.G. White, Pp.99, 106-107.

Younker, Randall W., God's Creation, *Sabbath School*, Personal Ministries Dept.; Silver Spring, MD, July-Sept, 1999, Pp.101-112.

Rehwinkel, Alfred M., *The Flood*, Concordia Publishing House, Saint Louis, Missouri, 1951, Copyright 1951 by Concordia Publishing House, Pp.177-187.

Morris, Henry M., *Science and the Bible*, Moody Press, Chicago, 1986, © 1951, by Henry M. Morris, Pp.63-66; 79-81.

Marsh, Frank Lewis, *Life, Man, and Time*, Published by Outdoor Pictures, Escondido, CA, 1967, Pp.97-115.

Genesis, Chapters 1-11; 6:12, 13, 15, 17; 7:1-4, 11, 18-22, 9:13-15.

QUESTION FIVE

Morris, John & Ham, Ken, Illustrated by Jonathan Chong; *What Really Happened to the Dinosaurs?* Master Books, A Division of CLP, Inc., El Cajon, CA, Copyright © 1988, 1990, P.22.

Unfred, David, *Dinosaurs and the Bible*, Huntington House Publishers, Lafayette, LA, Copyright © 1990 by David W. Unfred, cover and interior art copyright © 1990 by David W. Unfred, P.9.

Taylor, Paul S., *The Great Dinosaur Mystery and the Bible*, Accent Publications, Inc., Denver, Colorado, copyright © 1987,1989, Paul S. Taylor and Films for Christ Association, Tenth Printing 1991, P.32.

Ibid. *Life, Man, and Time*, Pp.106, 156.

Wheeler, Ruth & Coffin, Harold G., *Dinosaurs*, Pacific Press Publishing Association, P.24.

Genesis 6:19-20; 7:15 -16

QUESTION SIX

(Roland T. Bird, *Natural History*, May 1939, Pp.255-56. Quoted in "Man's Origin, Man's Destiny" by A.E. Wilder-Smith, P.137).

Ritland, Richard M., *A Search for Meaning in Nature*, Pacific Press Publishing Association, Mountain View, California, 1970, copyright © 1970 by Pacific Press Publishing Association, P.230, 232.

Wilder-Smith, A.E., *Man's Origin, Man's Destiny*, Bethany House Publishers, Minneapolis, Minnesota, A Division of Bethany Fellowship, Inc., copyright, 1968, P.137.

Whitcomb, JR., John C. & Morris, Henry M., *The Genesis Flood*, The Presbyterian and Reformed Publishing Company, Philadelphia, Penna., copyright, 1961, Pp. 174-175.

Hayward, Alan, *Creation and Evolution*, 1985, copyright © Alan Hayward, Minneapolis, Minnesota, Bethany House Publishers, P.149.

QUESTION SEVEN

Pittack, Richard B., *The Archaeopteryx Controversy*, Chapter Twelve, Section (2) Dinosaur Graveyards.

QUESTION EIGHT

Woodmorappe, John, *Studies in Flood* Geology, second edition, El Cajon, California, © 1999 by *The Institute for Creation Research*, P.16.

Genesis 6:14

QUESTION NINE

Ibid. *The Flood*, Pp.221-237.

Cohen, Daniel and Susan, *Where to Find Dinosaurs Today*, Cobblehill Books, New York, New York, 1992, copyright © 1992 by Daniel and Susan Cohen, Pp.136-137.

Colbert, Edwin H., *The Great Dinosaur Hunters and Their Discoveries*, Dover Publications, Inc., New York, Copyright © 1968, 1984 by Edwin H. Colbert, Pp.154-162.

QUESTION TEN

Ojakangas, Richard W., *Theory and Problems of Introductory Geology*, Schaum's Outline Series, New York, Copyright © 1991 by McGraw-Hill, Inc., Pp.49-63.

Clark, Harold W., *Fossils, Flood, and Fire*, Outdoor Pictures, Escondido, California, Copyright, 1968, Harold W. Clark, Pp.29-36.

Morris, Henry M., *Science and the Bible,* Revised and Updated, Moody Press, Chicago, © 1986, by Henry Morris, Pp.63-88.

QUESTION ELEVEN

Matthew 24:37-39

John: 46-47

Hebrews 11:7

1 Peter 3:20

11 Peter 2:5; 3:3-7

QUESTION TWELVE

Lessem, Don, *Kings of Creation*, Illustrated by Jon Sibbick, Simon & Schuster, New York, New York, Copyright © 1992 by Don Lessem, P.11.

QUESTION THIRTEEN

Oard, Michael, *Frozen in Time*, first printing: October 2004, Copyright © 2004 by Michael Oard, Pp.97-100.

Brett-Surman, Michael K. (Consultant Editor), *A Guide to Dinosaurs*, Published by Fog City Press, San Francisco, CA, copyright © 2000 Weldon Owen Inc., P.145.

QUESTION FOURTEEN

"Beginning and Belongings," Page 15, (Adult Sabbath School Guide Oct-Nov-Dec 2006).

DeSalle, Rob & Lindley, David, *The Science of Jurassic Park* and *The Lost World*, Basic Books, A Division of Harper Collins Publishers, copyright © 1997 by Rob DeSalle and David Lindley.

Genesis 1:24-27

Exodus 20:11

Leviticus 19:19

QUESTION FIFTEEN

Ibid. *Studies in Flood Geology*, Pp.57-61.

White, E.G., *Steps to Christ*, Review and Herald, copyright, 1908 by Ellen G. White, P.67,

Ibid. *Patriarchs and Prophets*, P.264.

Genesis 1:24-27; 7:2

Ibid. *Life, Man, and Time*, Pp. 105-106.

QUESTION SIXTEEN AND SEVENTEEN

The Westminster Dictionary of the Bible, The Westminster Press, Philadelphia, copyright 1944, by The Westminster Press, P.64.

White, E.G., *Selected Messages Four*, Review and Herald Publishing Association, Washington, D.C., Copyright © 1968 by the Trustees of the Ellen G. White Publications, P.121.

Franklin, Linda, *Associated Press*, Oklahoma City, University of Oklahoma, "Paleontologists discover new, gigantic species of dinosaur."

Genesis 6:17-20

Genesis 7:14-16

Job 40:15-24

Malachi 9:3

QUESTION EIGHTEEN

Physical Geology by Chester R. Longwell, Adolph Knopf, and Richard F. Flint, Third Edition, New York, John Wiley & Sons, Inc. London, Chapman & Hall, Limited, Copyright, 1948 by Longwell, Knopf, and Flint, P.569.

(Berlitz, C. 1984. Atlantis, *The Eighth Continent*. New York. (Putnam quoted by Mark Isaak in "The Counter-Creationism Handbook" P.242).

Ibid. *The Counter-Creationism Handbook* by Mark Isaak, University of California Press, (Berkeley. Los Angeles. London} copyright © 2005 and 2007 by Mark Isaak. (Isaak quotes M. Polidoro, P.242).

The Billy Lids, The Mysterious Ica Stones, In Storytime, on the Billy Lids. Pp.1-5 (See http://www. bestoday. com.au/billylids/archives/000704the mysterious ica stones.php).

QUESTION NINETEEN

Dr. Dennis Swift, http://en.wikipedia.org/wiki/Acambaro figures.

Blanton, John, *The Acambaro Dinosaurs*, "Metareligion," Oct.1999.

Ibid. *Patriarchs and Prophets*, Pp.107-108.

Dr. Dennis Swift Ph.D,^http://www.bible.ca/tracls/tracks-acombaro.htm.

Benton, Michael, *Dinosaurs and other Prehistoric Animal Fact Finder*, Kingfisher Books, New York, © Grisewood 7 Dempsey Ltd. 1988, 1989, 1992 Text Prehistoric Animals © Michael Benton 1989, P.92.

Ibid. *The Counter-Creationism Handbook*, P.92.

Norman, David, *The Illustrated Encyclopedia of Dinosaurs*, Colour restorations by John Sibbick, published by Crescent Books, New York, © Salamander Books Ltd 1985, Pp.198-199.

QUESTION TWENTY

Gardom, Tim and Milner, Angela, *The Book of Dinosaurs the Natural History Museum Guide*, Prima Publishing, Rocklin, CA, copyright © 1993 Carlton Books, Limited, P.25, 94.

Lessem, Don, *Time for Learning Dinosaurs*, Peter Dodson Consultant, Illustrator, Phil Wilson, copyright © 2004 Publications International, Ltd., P.11.

Edited by Sylvia J. Czerkas and Everett C. Olson, *Dinosaurs Past and Present* (Volume ll), Natural History Museum of Los Angeles County in association with University of Washington Press Seattle and London, © 1987 by the Natural History Museum Foundation, P.66.

Genesis 1:24-25

JOB 3:8; 41

Psalms 74:14; 104:26

Isaiah 27:1

QUESTION TWENTY-ONE

Pittack, Richard B., *The Archaeopteryx Controversy,* Published by Walden's Computer Services.

QUESTION TWENTY-TWO

Czerkas, Sylvia J. and Czerkas, Stephen A., *Dinosaurs a Global View*, First published by Dragon's World 1990, © Dragon's World Ltd 1990 © test Sylvia J. and Stephen A. Czerkas 1990 © Colour Artwork resided with the individual artists 1990, Pp.104-109, 184.

Sunset magazine of June 1987, "Dinosaur Country" of *Coelophysis*, Pp.84-88, *Camarasaurus* and *Iguanodon*, P.90.

Ibid. *Dinosaurs,* Pp.65-67.

Ibid. *The Great Dinosaur Hunters and Their Discoveries*, Pp.186-187

QUESTION TWENTY-THREE

Pittack, Richard B., *The Archaeopteryx Controversy*, Published by Walden's Computer Services, copyright © 2007 by Richard B. Pittack.

Charig, Alan, *A New Look At the Dinosaurs*, Facts on File, Inc. New York, New York, copyright © 1979, 1983 British Museum (Natural History), Pp.26, 68.

National Geographic, July 1998, "Dinosaurs Take Wing," (Sinosauropteryx prima), THE ORIGIN OF BIRDS, Pp.81-83.

Ibid. *The Archaeopteryx Controversy*, Chapter Nine, "China and the Dinosaur-Bird Connection," (Do Feathered Dinosaurs Truly Exist?).

QUESTION TWENTY-FOUR

National Geographic, July 1998, Vol. 194. No.1. Article written by Jennifer Ackerman and entitled "Dinosaurs Take Wing."

QUESTION TWENTY-FIVE

Ibid. *The Book of Dinosaurs the Natural History Museum Guide*, Pp.41-43.

Lambert, David, *The Ultimate Dinosaur*, Dorling Kindersley, copyright © 1993 Dorling Kindersley Limited, London Text Copyright © 1993 David Lambert.

Ibid. *A New Look at the Dinosaurs,* P.104.

Ibid. *The Illustrated Encyclopedia of Dinosaurs*, Pp.68-73.

Ibid. *Dinosaur and Other Prehistoric Animal Fact Finder*, P.239.

QUESTION TWENTY-SIX

Isaiah 11:6-9; 65:25

Matthew 6:25-26

Luke 12:22-24

Romans 8:20, 22

QUESTION TWENTY-SEVEN

Genesis 1:29-30; 6:12

QUESTION TWENTY-EIGHT

Coffin, Harold, *Earth Story*, Review and Herald Publishing Association, Washington, DC, 1977, copyright © 1977 by the Department of Education, General Conference of Seventh-day Adventists.

Edited by John M. Harris and George T. Jefferson, *Treasures of the Tar Pits*, Science Series 31, © 1985 by The Natural History Museum Foundation, Pp.1-17.

Stock, Chester, *Rancho La Brea A Record of Pleistocene Life in California*, Los Angeles County Museum of Natural History, Science Series No.20, Paleontology, No.11, Seventh Printing, 1972, Pp.13-17.

QUESTION TWENTY-NINE

READERS DIGEST, *Mysteries of the Unexplained*, The Reader's Digest Association, Inc., Pleasantville, New York, Copyright © 1982, The Reader's Digest Association, Inc., Pp.149-151.

Ibid. *Quest for the African Dinosaurs*, Pp.243-265.

P. Jerlstrom and B. Elliott, "Let Rotting Sharks Lie: Further evidence for shark identity of the Zuiyo-Maru Carcass," CEN Technical Journal 13 (2); 83-87, 1999.

Ibid. *Counter-Creationism Handbook*, P100. (Native quote taken from R. O'Hanlon's book, *No Mercy: A Journey to the Heart of the Congo*, New York: Knopf, 1997, P.373).

QUESTION THIRTY

Morris, Henry M. and Morris, John D., *The Modern Creation Trilogy: Scripture and Creation*, Volume One, "Dragons in Paradise," copyright © 1996 by Master Books, Pp.207-212.

Job 30:29

Psalms 74:12-14

Micah1:3

Malachi 1:3

Revelation 12:3, 9, 13:4

QUESTION THIRTY-ONE

Gish, Duane T., *Dinosaur by Design*, Edited by Gloria Clanin, Illustrated by Earl & Bonita Snellenberger, Master Books, AR, copyright © 1992, Pp.82-83.

Bakker, Robert T., *The Dinosaur Heresies*, Zebra Books, Kensington Publishing Corp., copyright © 1986 by Robert T. Bakker, Illustrations copyright © 1986 by Robert T. Bakker, Pp.43, 345.

Genesis 1:1-2:3

Job 3:3, 8; 41:18-21

Revelation 9:17-18

QUESTION THIRTY-TWO

Ibid. *Dinosaurs by Design,* P.82.

Job 41:18-21

Revelation 9:17-18

QUESTION THIRTY-THREE

Ibid. *Fossils, Flood, and Fire*, Pp.91-104.

Clark, Harold W., *Genesis and Science*, Southern Publishing Association, Nashville, Tennessee, Copyright © 1967 by Southern Publishing Association, Pp.93-95.

Ibid. *The Genesis Flood*, Pp.162-165.

Ibid. *Earth Story*, Pp.133-135.

Peterson, W. 1924. Dinosaur tracks in the roof of coalmines. *Natural History*, 24 (3):388. (Peterson's description is found in Harold G. Coffin's book, *Creation-Accident or Design*, Pp.77-78.

QUESTION THIRTY-FOUR

Shimer, John A., *This Sculptured Earth,* Columbia University Press, New York, 1959, Copyright © 1959 by Columbia University Press.

Ibid. *The Genesis Flood*, Pp.370-378.

Ibid. *Treasures of the Tar Pits*, Pp.7-9.

Ibid. *Life, Man, and Time*, Pp.56-68.

Ibid. *Man's Origin Man's Destiny*, Pp.116-127.

Bates, Robert L. & Jackson, Julia A., *Dictionary of Geological Terms*, Doubleday, New York, 1976, copyright, © 1984 by the American Geological Institute.

Clark, Harold W., *The Battle Over Genesis*, Review and Herald Publishing Association, Washington, D.C. 1977, copyright © 1977 by Review and Herald Publishing Association.

Zimmerman, Paul A., *Darwin, Evolution, and Creation*, Concordia Publishing House, Saint Louis, Missouri, 1959, Copyright 1959 by Concordia Publishing Association, Pp. 156-166.

QUESTION THIRTY-FIVE

Ibid. *Darwin, Evolution, and Creation*, Pp.145-156.

Gentry, Robert V., *Creation's Tiny Mystery*, Earth Science Associates, Knoxville, Tennessee, 1992, Third Edition, © 1992 by Robert V. Gentry, 109-115.

Ibid. *A New Look At Dinosaurs*, Pp.34-36.

Parker, Steve and Bernor, Raymond L., Editor, *The Practical Paleontologist*, Simon & Schuster Inc., 1990, Copyright © 1990 by Quarto Publishing pic., Pp.24-25.

Ibid. *Life, Man, and* Time, Pp.42-56.

Lambert, David, & The Diagram Group, *The Dinosaur Data Book*, Avon Books, New York, New York, 1990, Copyright © 1990 by David Lambert and Diagram Visual Information Ltd. Published by arrangement with Diagram Visual Information Ltd., Pp.224-225.

McGowan, Christopher, *Dinosaurs, Spitfires, & Sea Dragons*, Harvard University Press, Cambridge, Massachusetts, 1991, Copyright © 1991 by Christopher McGowan, P.295.

Ibid. *Quest for the African Dinosaurs*, P.28.

Comninellis, Nicholas, *Creative Defense* (Evidence against Evolution), printed by Master Books, Copyright © 2001 By Master Books, Inc., Pp.115-116.

Morris, Henry M. & Morris, John D., *The Modern Creation Trilogy*, Volume Two, second printing: November 1997, Copyright © 1996 by Master Books, Pp.324-326.

QUESTION THIRTY-SIX

Paul, Gregory S., *Predatory Dinosaurs of the World*, (A New York Academy of Sciences Book written and drawn by Gregory S. Paul), A Touchstone Book published by Simon & Schuster Inc., New York, Copyright © 1988 by Gregory S. Paul, Pp.78-83.

Ibid. *The Book of Dinosaurs*, Pp.78-87.

Ibid. *The Dinosaur Heresies*, Pp.425-444.

Ibid. *Quest for the African Dinosaurs*, Pp.158-163.

Ibid *A New Look at the Dinosaurs*, Pp.149-151.

Powell, James Lawrence, *Night Comes to the Cretaceous*, Harcourt Brace & co., New York, 1988, Copyright © 1998 by James Lawrence Powell, Pp.125-141.

Michard, Jean-Guy, *The Reign of the Dinosaurs*, Harry N. Abrams, Inc., Publishers New York, 1992, English translation copyright © 1992 by Harry N. Abrams, Inc., Pp.85-95.

Ibid. *Kings of Creation*, Pp.287-305.

Ibid. *Hunting Dinosaurs*, Pp.255-259

Ibid. *Dinosaurs, Spitfires, & Sea Dragons* Pp. 291-311.

Ibid. *The Dinosaur Data Book*, Pp.34-35.

Ibid. *The Hot-Blooded Dinosaurs*, Pp.184-197.

Ibid. *The Ultimate Dinosaur*, Pp.24-25.

Ibid. *Dinosaurs A Global View*, Pp.234-237.